MW00576307

Elizabeth of the Trinity
Her Life and Spirituality

Elizabeth holding her profession crucifix

Elizabeth of the Trinity Her Life and Spirituality

The Vast Triangled Heart

Marian T. Murphy, O.C.D.

GRACEWING

First published in 2011

Gracewing
2 Southern Avenue
Leominster
Herefordshire HR6 0QF

All rights reserved. No part of this publication may be reproduced, stored in a retrieval system, or transmitted in any form, or by any means, electronic, mechanical, photocopying, recording or otherwise, without the written permission of the publisher.

© Marian T. Murphy, O.C.D.

The right of Marian T. Murphy, O.C.D. to be identified as the author of this work has been asserted in accordance with the Copyright, Designs and Patents Act 1988.

ISBN 978 0 85244 728 4

Typeset by Action Publishing Technology Ltd,
Gloucester GL1 5SR

To
Susan, John, Gemma, Sian
and
Suzannah Marian
with all my love and prayer

The whole world round is not enough to fill
The heart's three corners but it craveth still.
Only the Trinity who made it can
Suffice the vast triangled heart of man.
The School of the Heart
B. Haevten

Contents

Acknowledgements

My wholehearted thanks are due to all those who have made it possible for this book to be written, through their prayers and support, and to Fr Frank for his Mass intentions.

A special word of gratitude to my prioress, Mother Mary of the Incarnation, who first suggested I study Elizabeth of the Trinity as the subject of my MA dissertation, to mark her Centenary Year, Trinity Sunday 2006–2007. Thanks too for her careful readings of the manuscript, thoughtful suggestions and unstinting love and support. Thanks also to each sister in my Carmelite Community in Liverpool who gave me the time, prayer and loving encouragement to complete this book.

Thanks also to the community of Dijon-Flavignerot Carmel, for their support and prayer, and for permission to use pictures of Elizabeth and extracts from private publications.

A special word of appreciation to all those who, on discovering Elizabeth have responded to her life and message with such heart-warming enthusiasm, and who have made her prayer their own.

Sincere thanks to Tom Longford for his trust, confidence and patience. May his Gracewing apostolate of life-giving works continue to flourish.

The greatest thanks of all, however, go to Elizabeth of the Trinity, whose longing for the God of Love, insights into the mystery of the indwelling Trinity and fidelity to grace, have changed my life.

Abbreviations

1A	Ascent of Mount Carmel, Bk 1
2A	Ascent of Mount Carmel, Bk 2
3A	Ascent of Mount Carmel, Bk 3
C	Spiritual Canticle
CCC	Catechism of the Catholic Church
CWJC	Complete Works of John of the Cross
D	Diary of Elizabeth
EDC	Elizabeth of the Trinity's Death Circular
EdE	Ecclesia de Eucharistia
GOS	Gift of Scripture
GS	Gaudium et Spes
GV	Greatness of Our Vocation
HF	Heaven in Faith
IC	Interior Castle
L	Letter of Elizabeth
LF	Living Flame of Love
LG	Lumen Gentium
Life	Life of St Teresa of Avila
LOH	Liturgy of the Hours, vols I–III
LR	Last Retreat of the 'Praise of Glory'
MF	Mysterium Fidei
NMI	Novo Millennio Inuente
OC	Oeuvres Complètes
P	Poem of Elizabeth
PN	Personal Notes of Elizabeth
SD	Salvifici Doloris
Way	Way of Perfection

Introduction

I think that in heaven my mission
will be to draw souls by helping them
go out of themselves to cling to God
by a wholly simple and loving movement,
and to keep them in this great silence within
that will allow God to
communicate Himself to them
and transform them
into Himself.[1]

'Lived Theology' of the Saints

We all love stories, especially about people who overcome
unimaginable difficulties, or demonstrate great courage in
succeeding against the odds; their resilience and nobility inspire
us to become better human beings. They fascinate us because they
alert us to our tremendous potential, resonating within our very
being which cries out for greatness, and this is just on a human
level. When it comes to the spiritual dimension, the possibilities
are limitless, and that is where the saints come into their own.
While concepts and doctrine are important, we respond more
eagerly to the dynamic witness of holy people, the 'lived theology' of the saints.[2] In their lives, we see God in action. A saint is
one of God's 'success' stories; an ordinary human being, for even
the best of God's saints is but a poor mixed being but one who,
through the grace of God and their own persevering response,
achieved holiness. The greatest tragedy in life is to waste this
potential, to 'have the experience and miss the meaning'.[3]

Holiness – Our Absolute Vocation

God's graced call to holiness is not an optional extra in life, it is
actually the whole point of our existence, holiness is our absolute
vocation; for this we are made. This realization led Leon Bloy to
write the haunting sentence, 'There is only one sadness, the
sadness of not being a saint.'[4] The call to sanctity expresses itself
in several distinct ways: the first call to be a Christian; the specific
call for each person, which defines one's purpose and mission in
life, and the immediate call to fulfil life's tasks in the present
moment.

From New Testament times, we have spontaneously honoured
the *hagios,* the holy ones, who have followed Christ so closely
that, as the *Catechism of the Catholic Church* says, they have become
models, companions and guides for those of us who are still on
the Christian pilgrimage. Their varied spiritualities offer Christians assistance suited to different needs, temperament and
culture. We study the saints because 'they are refractions of the
one pure light of the Holy Spirit' whose radiance attracts and
inspires us to love God more.[5]

> 'The saints have always been the source and origin of renewal in
> the most difficult moments of the Church's history.' Indeed,
> 'holiness is the hidden source and infallible measure of the
> Church's apostolic activity and missionary zeal.'[6]

The saints are God's glorious palette, and without them, as
Chesterton said, we could lose the humanity of Christ and his
rootedness in our ordinary lives.

The Power of Grace

Thomas Merton initially found Thérèse of Lisieux an improbable
saint, coming as she did from a 'stuffy, overplush' bourgeois
background. When he eventually penetrated beyond his misap-
prehension and discovered the real Thérèse, he was shocked by
his underestimation of the power of grace. He never stopped
thanking God for such a 'big present' and his appreciation for the
gift of St Thérèse lies behind his enthusiastic reflection:

It is a wonderful experience to discover a new saint. For God is greatly magnified and marvellous in each one of his saints: differently in each individual one. There are no two saints alike: but all of them are like God, like Him in a different and special way. In fact, if Adam had never fallen, the whole human race would have been a series of magnificently different and special images of God, each one of all the millions of people showing forth His glories and perfections in an astonishing new way, and each one shining with his own particular holiness, a holiness destined for him from all eternity as the most complete and unimaginable supernatural perfection of his human personality.[7]

Elizabeth of the Trinity, a near contemporary of Thérèse, has also been misunderstood. Some have found her rather serious, too perfect, her language and spirituality too exalted and, therefore, unattainable. She would not recognize herself in this at all, for the real Elizabeth was an attractive, fashion-conscious young woman, a talented musician with all the richness, flaws and struggles of her artistic temperament, passionate to the core. Her 'iron will' and ardent heart were given to God from an early age so that she shows us, in her own unique way, what 'complete love, complete trust, complete confidence look like' and she offers, 'not only an example but an outstretched hand' that pulls us up to share her vision of holiness.[8]

Elizabeth of the Trinity

Unlike St Thérèse, whose *Autobiography* catapulted her to fame, Elizabeth of the Trinity has only slowly become known, perhaps because Elizabeth's spirituality of silence, prayer and deep inner life with God are so needed today. We derive our knowledge of her from poems, personal notes and the remains of her diary, but mainly from her letters. Cardinal Newman said that a person's life lies in their letters. Mother Germaine, her Prioress and first biographer, claimed that Elizabeth could only be intimately known through her letters, which vividly convey her rich personality and loving nature; through them, we encounter Elizabeth face to face. Her letters to her mother and sister unselfconsciously express an intense love for her family. As we come to know Elizabeth more fully, we begin to fathom the depths of her holiness. Elizabeth writes beautiful prose, which often becomes poetic as she pours out her soul with great simplicity and serenity. Indeed, her writings contain a wealth of spiritual insights and wisdom, which is why I have used her own words where possible.

In Elizabeth's short life she managed to pack in a lot of learning, loving and growing. She was twenty-one when she entered Carmel and only twenty-six when she died. John of the Cross says that God characteristically takes to himself those who love him ardently, because, in a very short space of time, he perfects them through that love.[9] Elizabeth fulfilled the goal of every person's life, expressed in response to the inescapable question which comes to us all, *What's it all about?* This central question is answered simply and profoundly in the old *Penny Catechism*, 'God made me to know, love and serve him in this world and be happy with him forever in the next'. Early on, Elizabeth grasped that we only become truly happy when we let God deeply into our lives. We are each called to holiness, for 'the glory of God is man fully alive'.[10] This astonishing insight into the deepest purpose of life challenges us, calling us to fullness of life.

'Look into the soul of the saints'

In the Prologue of *The Living Flame,* John of the Cross wrote, 'everything I say is as far from the reality as is a painting from the living object represented'.[11] This is true about this book on Elizabeth which attempts to arouse our interest in and enthusiasm for this beautiful saint. Elizabeth's life is its own recommendation and her holiness is profoundly inspiring. I encourage you to let the Holy Spirit touch you through her and to 'join me in praying to her every day for the wisdom that makes saints and brings the soul great peace and happiness.'[12] She actually wrote these words to a friend, referring to Thérèse of Lisieux, never dreaming that one day they would be used of her. As we enter deeply into the soul of this young saint and listen to her life and words, let us take something from what we read and become something of what we learn. Let her words be our way into her life and spirituality:

It is good for us to look into the soul of the saints and to follow
them, in faith, right up to heaven. There they shine with the light
of God, whom they contemplate face to face. This heaven of the
saints is our homeland, the Father's house, where we are awaited
and loved, and where, one day, we too will fly and rest in the
bosom of Infinite Love. When we fix our eyes on the divine world
which already surrounds us, even in our earthly exile, then the
things of this world simply disappear! They are the things that are
not, they are less than nothing. The saints fully understood this
true wisdom, which makes us leave all things, ourselves above all,
to fly to God and dwell in Him alone. He dwells in us to make us
holy. Let us ask Him to be Himself our holiness.[13]

Notes
1. *L* 335.
2. *NMI* 27.
3. Eliot, 'The Dry Salvages', *Four Quartets*, l. 93.
4. Nicholl, *Holiness*, p. 28.
5. *CCC* 2684.
6. *CCC* 828.
7. Merton, *Elected Silence*, p. 34.
8. Balthasar, *Two Sisters,* p. 417.
9. *LF* 1.34.
10. St Irenaeus, *Adv. haeres.* 4, 20, 7 in *CCC* 294.
11. *LF* Prol 1.
12. *L* 249.
13. *L* 184.

Chronology

1880	18 July	Born in military barracks Camp d'Avor, near Bruges, in central France, to Joseph and Marie Catez.
	22 July	Baptized Marie Joséphine Elizabeth Catez.
1882	9 May	Grandmother, Mme Rolland, dies in Saint-Hilaire, and her grandfather, Commandant Rolland, comes to live with them.
	1 Nov.	The family moves to Dijon.
1883	20 Feb.	Marguerite (Guite) is born.
1887	24 Jan.	Commandant Rolland dies.
	2 Oct.	Captain Catez, aged 54, dies of a heart attack.
		They move to Prieur-de-la-Côte-d'Or, near the Dijon Carmel.
		Elizabeth makes her First Confession.
1888	October	Elizabeth is enrolled in the Dijon Conservatory of Music.
1891	19 April	First Holy Communion at St Michael.
	8 June	Confirmation at Notre-Dame.
1893	18 July	First prize for Excellence in Higher Fundamentals of Music.
	25 July	First prize for Piano.
1894		Private vow of perpetual virginity. Feels interior call to 'Carmel'.
1897		Elizabeth formally asks permission to enter Carmel, but Madame Catez still refuses.
1899	26 March	Palm Sunday, Mme Catez agrees to Eliz-

		abeth entering Carmel when she is twenty-one.
		Elizabeth reads and is greatly influenced by Sr Thérèse of Lisieux's *Story of a Soul*.
1901	2 August	First Friday, Elizabeth enters Carmel.
	8 Dec.	Elizabeth receives the Carmelite habit.
1902	Aug.–Sept.	Meets Abbé Andre Chevignard, Georges' brother, a twenty-three-year-old seminarian.
	15 Oct.	Marguerite marries Georges Chevignard.
	22 Dec.	Canonical examination before profession.
		Elizabeth spends time outside enclosure with her mother and sister.
1903	1–10 Jan.	Personal retreat in preparation for profession.
	11 Jan.	Epiphany Sunday, Elizabeth makes her religious profession.
	21 Jan.	Feast of St Agnes, Elizabeth receives black veil.
		Some time in 1903, Elizabeth is diagnosed with Addison's Disease.
1904	11 March	Birth of Elizabeth Chevignard, Guite's first child, who eventually entered the Dijon Carmel as Sr Elizabeth of Jesus, d. 1991.
	21 Nov.	Feast of the Presentation, Elizabeth writes *Prayer to the Trinity* which is found only after her death.
1905	8 Mar.–22 Apr.	Lent: Addison's Disease begins to take hold. Dispensations from the Rule.
	19 April	Birth of Odette Chevignard, her second niece.
	August	Relieved of turn duties, rests in garden.
1906	c. 19 March	Elizabeth is moved (permanently) to the infirmary.
	8 April	Palm Sunday, Elizabeth is dying and receives the Last Sacraments.

13 April	Good Friday, she is critical again.
14 April	Holy Saturday, unexpected improvement.
13 May	Another serious attack, once again they think she is dying.
8/9 July	After invoking Thérèse of Lisieux's help, Elizabeth is able to walk again.
August	*Greatness of our Vocation*, final letter written to Françoise de Sourdon.
Early Aug.	*Heaven in Faith,* a ten-day souvenir retreat for Guite.
16–31 Aug.	*Last Retreat*, notes on her 'noviciate for heaven'.
Oct./Nov.	*Let Yourself Be Loved*, letter to Mother Germaine, found after her death.
29 Oct.	Last visit from Elizabeth's family.
9 Nov.	Elizabeth dies, after only 5 years in Carmel.
1931 23 Mar./May	Cause for her Beatification and Canonization introduced.
1961 25 Oct.	John XXIII gives papal approval.
1984 17 Feb.	Miracle attributed to the intercession of Sr Elizabeth is given papal approval. Fr Jean Chanut, a Cistercian with TB, was completely healed after a novena of prayer to Sr Elizabeth offered by his own abbey of Citeaux and other Cistercian communities.
25 Nov.	Sr Elizabeth is beatified on the Solemnity of Christ the King, by Pope John Paul II.

Part I
Elizabeth's Life

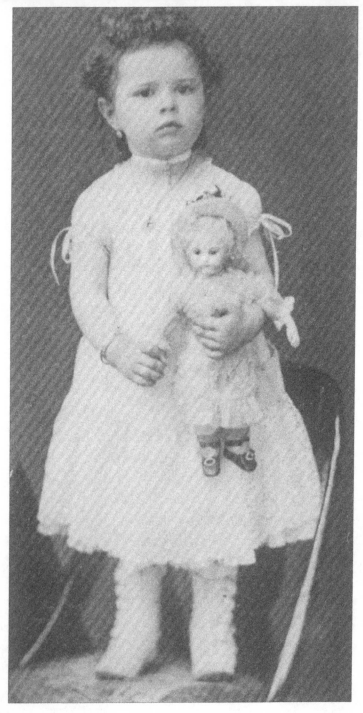

Elizabeth, aged 2

Chapter 1

A Child of Contrasts

'Blessed are they who . . . in their youth turn to Him.'
Cardinal John Henry Newman

Soldiers' Blood in Her Veins

Elizabeth's life began and ended in sacrament. When two doctors told a distraught Monsieur Catez that his wife and baby would not survive the birth, he rushed to the camp chaplain, begging him to offer Mass for a safe delivery. As the Mass ended, Elizabeth's life began. Marie Joséphine Elizabeth Catez was born on Sunday 18 July 1880, in an army camp in Avor near Bourges, in central France, into a military family on both sides. Elizabeth had the best possible start in life, because she was born to loving parents who shared a deep faith. Her father, Joseph Catez, of peasant stock, was a noble character, with a sociable temperament. A courageous army Captain, loved by his companions and respected by superiors, he was awarded the Military Medal and also made a Chevalier of the Legion of Honour. Her mother, Marie Rolland, the daughter of a Commandant, was of a strong and more serious disposition. Elizabeth, Sabeth, as she was affectionately known, inherited excellent qualities from both parents, while the soldiers' blood in her veins showed itself from an early age in her passionate, fiery temperament.

When the family eventually settled in Dijon in 1882, Elizabeth's maternal grandfather, Raymond Rolland, came to live with them after his wife died. There, Elizabeth's beloved sister and lifelong friend, Marguerite, Guite, for short, was born on 20 February 1883. The girls were both virtuous as well as charming, but whereas Elizabeth was exuberant and lively, Guite, in contrast, was so shy and serious that she was nicknamed 'Justice'.

A Child of Contrasts – Affectionate and Volatile

A warm and affectionate child, Elizabeth could also be extremely stubborn and self-willed; her ferocious temper was legendary. While Mme Catez was visiting her sick mother in St Hilaire, there was a service for the blessing of the children. Elizabeth's favourite doll, Jeannette, was borrowed and dressed up as the baby Jesus. When nineteen-month-old Elizabeth espied her beloved doll, she cried out, in a fit of rage, 'Jeanette! Give me back my Jeanette! You naughty priest you!' and had to be carried out of the church, by her nurse, to the amusement of the congregation, and embarrassment of her mother.

Despite her choleric temperament and angry outbursts, Elizabeth was a loving, sensitive child and Mme Catez wrote to her husband describing how Elizabeth kissed the crucifix and taught her doll, Jeanette, to kneel and pray for her sick grandmother. As time passed, however, her worried mother noted that Elizabeth's irascible temperament was worsening and people were alarmed by her furious eyes. Only later, when God had taken over, would these same eyes be admired for their calm and heavenly gaze.

1887, A Year of Grief and Grace

Passion turned to grief in 1887 as, within the space of nine months, the small Catez family was devastated by the loss of both grandfather and father. Elizabeth's doting grandfather, Raymond Rolland, died on 27 January. A marvellous storyteller, a gift which Elizabeth inherited from him, he amused the girls for hours with tales that fascinated and formed their minds and they worshipped him. Worse still, her beloved father died suddenly of a heart attack on Sunday morning, 2 October, aged only fifty-four. Elizabeth was with him when he died, and ten years later she commemorated his death with a poem which ends:

> It was in my weak child's arms
> Those arms that hugged you so
> That your brief agony lasted,
> Your life's last fight.
> I tried to hold on to
> That last, long sigh.[1]

These poignant lines give us a rare insight into how deeply bereavement affected Elizabeth, conveying the young daughter's love, longing and loss, and suggesting that he actually died in her arms. The distressing stages of grief have since been clearly identified by Kubler-Ross: denial, bargaining, anger, guilt, depression and acceptance. While there have been no clinical studies exploring the connection between the death of a parent and spiritual growth, it seems more than coincidence that several great Carmelite mystics lost a parent at an early age: Teresa of Avila was only twelve when her mother died; Thérèse was four; Edith Stein was not yet two and John of the Cross' father died only a few months after his birth. To have encountered mortality at such young ages must have marked them with a sense of the transitory nature of life, pushing them more deeply into God. Like many great saints, Elizabeth knew suffering from an early age and this experience laid deep foundations in her life. It may also explain her capacity to both endure and wholeheartedly embrace the appalling suffering of her terminal illness, when she was only twenty-six years old.

In the short term, however, Elizabeth's reactions were complex. The threefold experience of loss: of grandfather, father and change of home would have had an immense impact on this sensitive child. Feelings of anger which are a normal part of the grieving process must have put Elizabeth's naturally fiery temperament into overload and probably contributed to the 'absolutely real rages' which continued and intensified. These were so alarming that Mme Catez even packed Elizabeth's bag, threatening to put her in the nearby Good Shepherd Institute, which was a house of correction for young girls. However, Sabeth's greatest punishment was much more subtle: to be sent to bed without a goodnight kiss from her mother, a practice which Guite adopted with her own children, to great effect, according to her son, Jacques.

Their home was now too large for the reduced Catez family, the 'trio', as Madame Catez, Sabeth and Guite called themselves, so they moved to the Rue Prieur-de-la-Côte-d'Or on the other side of town. Their new apartment was only 200 metres from the Dijon Carmel and actually overlooked the garden.

My 'Conversion'

Elizabeth described her First Confession in 1887, as a 'conversion', a graced moment, enabling her to recognize, embrace and live her baptismal faith. Conversion, of fundamental importance for Christians, is the experience of God calling us to a profound change of heart. This *metanoia,* is usually characterized by a moral transformation and practical change in conduct, which cannot simply be attributed to human maturation. Some say that in prayer we find God, but more truly, it is God who finds us: grace always precedes the call. Conversion involves a willingness to change, which is 'the core of our response to God'.[2] While it can happen suddenly and dramatically, as famously recounted in St Augustine's *Confessions*, it often occurs gradually, and regular sacramental confession offers a source of ongoing grace. From an adult perspective, it appears startling for one so young to speak of her 'conversion'. Moreover, Elizabeth gives no details; was she referring to a spiritual awakening, described in terms of conversion? We can only conjecture; what is clear, however, is that at the time of her First Confession, Elizabeth consciously decided to respond to the grace of Christ and her spiritual life began in earnest.

As Elizabeth's relationship with God and her love of prayer developed, she wanted to give herself totally to him. Even from a young age she could not understand how anyone could give their heart to another. One day, while visiting their close family friend, Canon Angles, she hopped on to his knee and whispered, 'I want to be a nun!' Her mother was shocked and disapproving, firmly dismissing the possibility of her volatile daughter becoming a religious. Canon Angles, however, aware of Elizabeth's deepening prayer life, was convinced of Elizabeth's vocation and, indeed, of her holiness, carefully keeping all her letters, sensing that they might be needed.

Although Elizabeth made remarkable efforts to overcome her temper there were still explosive outbursts. She intuitively recognized the truth of the words of Horace, 'Anger is a momentary madness, so control your passion or it will control you.' Elizabeth knew what this felt like! The conversion process was evidently gradual, as several New Year letters to her mother confirm. She resolved to be a gentle, patient and obedient little girl and to refrain from losing her temper, especially as she was anticipating the happiness of making her First Communion soon, 'I will be even more well-behaved, and I'll pray to God to make me even better.'[3] It is heartening to learn that saints have to repeat their resolutions.

A Milestone – First Holy Communion

In his book, *Jesus of Nazareth*, Pope Benedict speaks of milestones in the spiritual life.[4] Elizabeth's First Holy Communion on 19 April 1891, at the age of ten years and nine months, was such a milestone, which she cherished as the most beautiful day of her life. Everyone was moved by her silent tears of joy which flowed throughout the Mass. The depth of her emotion reminds us of Gregory of Nyssa's words, 'It is impossible for one to live without tears who considers things as they really are.'[5] Elizabeth, like all mystics, had this perception of the wonder of Christ's gift in the Eucharist. As they left church, heading for the celebratory feast, Elizabeth confided to her best friend, Marie-Louise Hallo, 'I am not hungry; Jesus has fed me.'[6] Seven years later, she recalled the grace of her First Communion in a poem *This Great Day,* writing of a 'mysterious exchange' whereby 'we gave ourselves to each other without words.' The Lord took over her heart.[7]

Elizabeth – House of the God of Love

On the afternoon of her First Communion the trio visited Carmel, where Elizabeth received a prayer card of Teresa of Avila's sayings, on which the Prioress had written a short reflection explaining the significance of Elizabeth's name in Hebrew, 'House of God'. Little did she know that it would become the watchword of Elizabeth's spiritual life:

> Your blessed name holds a mystery
> Fulfilled this great day.
> Child, your heart, here on earth,
> Is the House of the God of Love.[8]

Elizabeth was deeply impressed by this as it confirmed what she had felt so strongly that morning when she received Jesus in the Eucharist for the first time, the God of Love was dwelling in her. She kept the card in her prayer book for the rest of her life. This interior sense of being the dwelling place of the God of Love is a major feature of her spirituality. An ironic touch is that Elizabeth actually means, 'God has sworn', but there are no mistakes with God and though etymologically inaccurate, it was theologically true. We know with our heads that through baptism, we become temples of the living, loving God, but for Elizabeth it was a knowing that was part of her being – an absolute conviction that permeated and transformed her. Life only truly begins when we know ourselves loved. For Elizabeth, to be was to be indwelt by a God of love, which is why prayer was essential, as it simply meant spending time with the indwelling God.

Ongoing Struggle – Sacramental Grace

Soon after her First Communion Elizabeth celebrated the sacrament of Confirmation, when the Holy Spirit gifted her with a personal Pentecost, strengthening her generous heart. The change wrought in her by these two sacraments was clear to all. Elizabeth's love for Jesus in the Eucharist communicated itself to others and gave her the strength to struggle against her passionate temperament and to practise virtue. Only Canon Angles knew what efforts she exerted in battling her impetuous nature and controlling her emotions, and also knew that these were fuelled by prayer and motivated by her love of Jesus.

A childhood friend, Louise Recoing, recounts an occasion when she and Elizabeth wanted their group to play different games. The situation was getting heated when, to Louise's complete surprise, Elizabeth capitulated, suggesting that they begin with Louise's game which would be 'much more fun than mine'. When Louise looked at her in amazement, she saw tears in Elizabeth's eyes, testifying to the effort it cost her to give in. Louise was both moved and impressed. What is particularly striking about this incident is that Elizabeth, although a natural leader, had caught herself trying to impose her will on others and succeeded in overcoming this tendency. Gifted as Elizabeth was with great sincerity and uprightness, once she resolved to grow in God, she applied herself assiduously to overcoming anything that would impede her, taking Ignatius' motto '*agendo contra*' (to go against herself) as her watchword.[9] Self-conquest became the law of her soul and there were often tears in her eyes as she fought back angry words and reactions.

In photographs taken at this time, Elizabeth's once angry eyes look peaceful as her gaze becomes purer and deeper. She responded wholeheartedly to God's grace working in her and the transformation went deep. She was still full of fun and high-spirits, but everyone remarked on how recollected she was in church.

Cardinal Newman, a man of the greatest integrity and wisdom, would have recognized a kindred spirit in Elizabeth. His words apply perfectly to her, 'Blessed are they who . . . give the flower of their days to Him.'[10] Indeed, much of what constitutes holiness for Newman is evident in Elizabeth: daily self-denial, averting temptation through prayer, the cultivation of serenity, dwelling in and acting from one's centre. Most importantly, perhaps, is their shared recognition that God is best honoured by 'absolute obedience to his call from within.'[11]

'A soul full of harmony'

Elizabeth's ardent temperament found a wonderful outlet in music. In October 1888, Mme Catez enrolled Elizabeth in the Dijon Conservatory of Music where she proved to be an extremely talented and hard-working musician, progressing so rapidly on the piano that, within the year, and despite being barely able to reach the pedals, she astounded the audience with a brilliant rendition of Steibelt's *The Storm*. While the piano demanded hours of disciplined application, music provided a broadening and refining influence, opening Elizabeth up to culture and channelling her passionate temperament, providing both creative self-expression and a calming influence. Martin Luther considered music a 'mistress of order' making people milder and gentler.

Mme Catez had her daughters educated at home by tutors, allowing more time to be devoted to music. Elizabeth's lack of formal education is evident in her shaky grammar and poor spelling, which would always follow their own rules. Her handwriting was so bad that, when she entered Carmel, she was given lessons by Sr Agnes. However, her musical aptitude more than made up for this.

In 1893, Elizabeth received the First Prize for Excellence and First Prize for Piano. Although she was deprived of the latter because of infighting among the staff, she accepted the injustice serenely. Local newspapers praised Elizabeth's sensitive and inspiring performances, making particular mention of Mendelssohn's *Caprice* and Liszt's *Second Rhapsody*. They predicted a great career in music for the 'brilliant Mademoiselle Catez'. Elizabeth loved all the romantic composers, especially Chopin, who invented the *ballade* and whose technically demanding masterpieces also emphasized expressive depth. Her young friend, Françoise de Sourdon, said Elizabeth played Chopin's Ballades with great 'sensitivity and soul'. The Hungarian Liszt, designated as perhaps the greatest pianist of all time, was also a great favourite. Elizabeth practised up to five hours a day, perfecting her technique and pouring her passionate heart into these exciting and exacting pieces, mastering the *Hungarian Rhapsody No. 2* when she was only fourteen! In order to prevent Elizabeth becoming vain, however, Mme Catez was sparing in her praise. Elizabeth was herself aware of the dangers of too much acclamation and asked God to prevent her from taking part in a concert if it would make her proud.

'You are the music while the music lasts'

Listeners retained enduring memories of Elizabeth's playing, touched by an indefinable inner quality which is hinted at in a beautiful photograph of Elizabeth, aged 13, sitting at the piano in the Gemeaux Chateau. A friend, Thérèse Renardet, who heard her playing a favourite piece, *Le Chant du Nautonier* (*The Song of the Boatman*) by Diémer, was enchanted. Elizabeth's evocative playing of the flowing arpeggios, expertly executed, mirrored the movement of the sea as waves cascade and tumble over each other. She recalled, 'Her whole body was moved by her soul . . . her body vibrated, but without exaggeration, all seemed measured as if she was guided by some inner music.'[12] Years later, when Thérèse visited a cove at *Belle-Ile-en-Mer*, where the waves crashed ceaselessly on the rocks, she recognized the dramatic landscape which Elizabeth's playing had so vividly evoked. It seemed that something inexpressible surfaced from the depths of her soul and spilled over into her playing in a very natural way, but with mysterious supernatural power, reminding us of Plato's reflection, 'Music and rhythm find their way into the secret places of the soul'. Elizabeth drew her listeners into those 'secret places' where they experienced:

> . . . music heard so deeply
> That it is not heard at all, but you are the music
> While the music lasts.[13]

Elizabeth entered so completely into her playing that she lost herself in it, becoming one with it. In the same way, she immersed herself in prayer, losing herself in God. For Elizabeth music was not just an extension of prayer, it was prayer: love seeking expression. She confided to a friend, 'When I can no longer pray, I play!' and 'Oh, how I used to love speaking to him that way!'[14]

When a friend admitted how nervous she was about performing in public, Elizabeth shared the secret of her own composure, revealing the depth of her intimacy with God, 'forget your audience and imagine you are alone with the divine Master.'[15] Elizabeth's advice takes us to a new level, towards a total focus on God and away from self which, paradoxically, liberates artist and instrument to transcend themselves. Elizabeth likened her soul to a lyre, 'under the mysterious touch of the Holy Spirit that he [might] draw from it divine harmonies.'[16] This is the secret of Elizabeth's playing and of her whole life, a secret which she shares with us: give yourself so totally to God and to each thing you do, however mundane or marvellous, and it will be transformed into something infinitely beautiful; this is living the sacrament of the present moment.

Elizabeth won First Prize for Piano at the Dijon Conservatory

A Physical and Moral Portrait

Life, however, was not all disciplined piano practice; neither did Elizabeth's serious efforts to work on herself make her at all dull. Far from it, she was a charming, vivacious young girl. A French Composition Exercise, 'My Physical and Moral Portrait', from November 1894, shows us her sense of humour and candour. She writes that her sparkling black eyes are somewhat spoiled by her thick eyebrows, which make her look rather stern and she is clearly self-conscious about her large feet. However, despite admitting to being 'somewhat scatterbrained', she does not hold grudges and considers herself a hard worker, with a cheerful disposition and a generally good character. While 'not being a model of patience', she feels she has reasonable mastery of herself and, most importantly, she has a good heart.[17]

Significantly, Elizabeth omits any reference to her considerable musical talent, intense spiritual life and love for Jesus. Her playful tone and ability to laugh at herself are appealing in their simplicity. Her sheer humanity is extremely attractive and she comes across as a very real young woman, one with whom we can identify.

'Silent music'

One day in 1894, just after receiving Holy Communion, Elizabeth heard the call of God within, that 'silent music' which John of the Cross describes as tranquil, quiet knowledge of the Beloved.[18] Elizabeth writes, 'I felt irresistibly urged to choose Him for my Bridegroom, and I bound myself to Him by a vow of perpetual virginity.'[19] All of this transpired without words. Possibly as a result of this grace, Elizabeth considered entering the Trappistines, drawn to this order because of its silence and austerity. However, several weeks later, also during thanksgiving after Communion, she heard the word 'Carmel' spoken within and her destination was decided. Little did Elizabeth suspect that her mother would oppose her religious vocation and that she would have to wait seven years before fulfilling her dream.

'The best of all mothers'

After God, Elizabeth's mother and sister were the two most significant people in her life and it is important, particularly at this pivotal point in Elizabeth's life, to understand something of her relationship with them.

Elizabeth's mother, née Marie Rolland, suffered great losses throughout her life. Tragically, her first fiancé, an officer, died during the War of 1870. The young and sensitive Marie was desolate and turned to God for consolation, even considering religious life. She enjoyed real happiness in her marriage to Joseph Catez in 1879. However, her mother died in 1882, and in 1887 she lost both her father and husband, leaving her on her own to care for two young daughters. Once, while on holiday, a viper bit her face. This severely altered her appearance and explains why photographs show her looking so old, more like Elizabeth's grandmother. Her health was permanently affected and, although a very strong character, she was never physically robust, which must have made her feel vulnerable and probably afraid of loneliness in her old age. At that time, moreover, it was usual for the eldest daughter to care for ageing parents, so it was natural to expect Elizabeth to be there for her. Drawn together by their tragic losses, the trio were understandably close. Mother and daughters were great friends and there is no record of Elizabeth ever having criticized her mother, a testament to her loyalty and love. In fact, she so esteemed her mother that after hearing a sermon on the training of children Elizabeth wrote, 'I have thanked God from the bottom of my heart for having given me such a mother; one who was gentle and at the same time severe, and could conquer my terrible character.'[20]

'The drama of two great loves'

Despite her mother's genuine piety and love for the great Teresa of Avila, she recoiled at the thought of her daughter becoming an enclosed Carmelite nun. Such was Elizabeth's respect and devotion for 'the best of all mothers', that she would not have considered entering Carmel without her permission. Mme Catez's resistance caused untold suffering to them both: Elizabeth could neither follow her vocation, nor could she share her growing spiritual life with the mother whom she loved 'to distraction'. Elizabeth turned to God in prayer, which was her strength and solace. She found time by rising regularly before dawn to spend an extra hour in prayer, by candlelight, but she had to conceal this from her mother, 'How many matches I had to dispose of in order to avoid awkward questions.'[21] What a world of suffering is hidden by this simple statement. Canon Angles, who knew both women intimately, described the conflict in Elizabeth's life, between God and her mother, as the 'drama of two great loves'. Notwithstanding her mother's opposition, Elizabeth continued to long for Carmel and to work on herself.

Writing after Elizabeth's death, Canon Angles conveys the power of her passionate personality and the 'twofold love' which helped to transform her:

> Elizabeth had all the more merit in that she was naturally lively, ardent and passionate. Born in a camp the daughter and granddaughter of officers, she felt the soldier's blood, hot and generous, coursing through her veins. She might easily have been hot-headed, self-willed, and fiery-tempered. Happily in her case, the vivacity was counter-balanced by a twofold love: love of her mother and love of God; of her mother, to whom she was utterly devoted and of Him whom she always named, in a tone that had something unearthly about it, 'Him'. Those large, beautiful eyes ... with their heavenly expression, were ceaselessly fixed upon her mother and God, constantly asking, 'What ought I to do?'[22]

However, once Elizabeth entered Carmel, her mother gradually accepted her vocation and as she rejoiced in her daughter's growing happiness, their intimacy deepened as they were once again able to share everything. Eventually, their roles were reversed as Elizabeth, with great simplicity, encouraged her mother along the path of prayer and holiness.

'Echo of my soul'

Elizabeth was very caring and always loved and nurtured her younger, more diffident sister, Guite. Elizabeth encouraged and supported her, trying to bring her out; they did everything together; photographs show their closeness. Guite was inconsolable when Elizabeth entered Carmel. The trio was no more. Guite wrote a heart-rending letter to their tutor Mlle Forey, pouring out her hurt and anger, which were more intensely felt because she tried to hide her feelings in order not to compound Mme Catez's suffering. Guite described the agony of the last days and the heartbreak, emptiness and loneliness which made her curse all convents. She felt, and sounded, 'broken'. With a candour characteristic of the Catez family, Guite acknowledged Elizabeth's suffering, describing her as wasting away from it.

Elizabeth also knew what her sensitive little sister Guite was suffering and did her utmost to maintain their intimacy, sharing everything about her new life, in letters and during regular visits, where Elizabeth's joy and evident happiness in Carmel proved a great consolation. They remained devoted to each other and it was to her little sister, 'the echo of my soul' that Elizabeth wrote some of her most beautiful and profound letters, sharing her deepest experiences of God, becoming in fact Guite's spiritual mother and guide.

Guite – First Witness to Elizabeth's Holiness

It is to Elizabeth that Guite credited her understanding of the interior life. Guite's firstborn, named after her aunt, also entered the Dijon Carmel, as Sr Elizabeth of Jesus. She said:

> Mama *lived* with her sister. She took all her advice. When you think how angry she was when Sr Elizabeth entered Carmel, how angry she was against all convents and what she became! She kept all of Elizabeth's letters, read them and re-read them.[23]

All Guite's children testified to their mother's tremendous prayer and extraordinary faith which 'always let her see God's love in all the events of her life, joyful or sad', even being widowed at forty-two and left impoverished to raise nine children on her own. The people of Dijon considered Guite a saint in her own right. [24]

Notes

1. *P* 37.
2. Hildebrand, *Transformation in Christ,* p. 28.
3. *L* 4, see *L* 5.
4. Benedict XVI, *Jesus of Nazareth*, p. 287.
5. Maloney, *Prayer of the Heart*, p. 89.
6. *Reminiscences*, p. 8.
7. *P* 47, *OC,* p. 958.
8. *Reminiscences*, p. 8.
9. Philipon, *Spiritual Doctrine*, pp. 7–8.
10. Newman, *Sermons* VIII, p. 243.
11. Murray Elwood, *Kindly Light*, p. 24. See Balthasar, *Two Sisters*, p. 454.
12. Dijon Carmel, *Amour Excessif,* DVD.
13. Eliot, 'The Dry Salvages', *Four Quartets*, l. 11.
14. *Reminiscences*, p. 16.
15. Ibid.
16. *HF* 43.
17. Moorcroft, *My Heaven*, p. 25.
18. *C* 15.25.
19. *Reminiscences*, p. 16.
20. Ibid., p. 17.
21. Ibid., p. 43.
22. Ibid., p. 8.
23. Kinney, 'Guite', pp. 26–43.
24. Ibid.

'The Trio'
Sabeth, age 10, and Guite, 8, with their mother

Chapter 2

Elizabeth in Exile

Friends of God
have always been trained and tested in the desert
not even Christ bypassed it.[1]

Testing of Spirits

The *Rule of St Benedict*, states that those who aspire to become monks should not be too readily admitted; in fact, they are to be 'left outside' for a few days, made to wait.[2] There is a significant spiritual principle at work here which, in traditional terminology, is referred to as 'testing the spirits', in order to ascertain if the vocation is genuine. If the candidate perseveres humbly, patiently and steadfastly in their desire to enter, then they are allowed in. Mme Catez's objection to her daughter's vocation meant that Elizabeth was 'left outside' for seven long years.

Crisis – Danger and Opportunity

This delay provoked a time of crisis, which the Chinese denote as *wei-ji*, danger and opportunity. It is ultimately a crossroad, a place of pain but also of possibility. Elizabeth could have responded in three ways: by abandoning her vocation, like the rich young man in Matthew's Gospel, by living passively, or by generously submitting to God's will. She chose the latter course, for she had grasped the secret of mature spirituality which, in the darkness of faith, recognizes that there are no accidents or interruptions in life; nothing is ever wasted. Elizabeth lived this painful reality with characteristic generosity and her unswerving fidelity to her

vocation during this long period made it one of the most spiritually productive of her life. Unable to enter Carmel, she chose to
make the long journey inward which is, in fact, the essence of the
spiritual journey.

The Strongest Principle of Growth Lies in Human Choice

The unattractive stubbornness of Elizabeth's earlier years developed into an impressive tenacity which suggests great spiritual
depth. One of the most important lessons we learn from Elizabeth's life, especially during this period of exile, is the interplay
between the limitlessness of God's grace and our personal choice
and responsibility. It is not what happens to us that determines
who we become, but how we choose to respond.

In order to understand the scope of our freedom, it is helpful
to distinguish between temperament, personality and character.
Temperament is what a person is born with, the raw material as
it were. Elizabeth was passionate, strong-willed and hypersensi-
tive. Personality is what develops through our interaction with
others, how we modify our natural tendencies to make ourselves
socially acceptable. Character, however, is what we choose to
be. It is the result of moment-by-moment choices which shape
who we are, which is why Thomas Aquinas insisted on the forma-
tion of good habits as the only basis for authentic Christian
virtue. We are, initially, our basic temperament; we often adopt
a persona or create a personality which makes us acceptable to
others, but we build our character by every choice we make.
This is liberating because we are free to become the person God
wants us to be. It is also challenging, as it requires constant vigi-
lance and hard work to keep on making good choices and
forming our character. Once we have understood the tremendous importance of our choices, we recognize the real meaning
of freedom and responsibility.

'Postulant outside the walls'

Throughout this period of waiting, which Elizabeth experienced as an exile, she courageously chose to follow her Carmelite vocation. Instead of being hidden in Carmel, Carmel was hidden in 'the cell of her heart',[3] especially during the first five years when her mother prohibited contact with Carmel. Only after 1899 were these restrictions lifted. By this time, so many young women wanted to join the fervent community of the Dijon Carmel that the enterprising Prioress, Mother Marie of Jesus, planned a new foundation in Paray-le-Monial. Meanwhile she trained them in the Carmelite spirit, involving them in the life and prayer of Carmel. They cleaned and decorated the chapel for feasts, sang for the liturgy and helped the extern sisters.[4] In short, they lived as Carmelites in the world, 'postulants outside the walls', while waiting to enter.[5]

Gift for Friendship

Elizabeth's happy character and spirit of faith helped her to remain positive during this long and difficult period and she steadfastly refused to succumb either to self-pity or resentment. Like all teenagers, she loved dancing, music, clothes and fashion. A skilful seamstress, she obtained 'ravishing material' and, expertly imitating the latest Paris fashions, created stunning hats and blouses; she herself had a particular weakness for gloves. There are photos of Elizabeth and her friends, striding along, arm in arm, wearing unbelievable hats.

Like Teresa of Avila, her spiritual guide, Elizabeth had a gift for friendship and a capacity for making herself loved. Affectionate and sociable by nature, Elizabeth was noted for her kindness and sensitivity. Her uprightness and loyalty made her a valued friend, as she never spoke ill of anyone, neither did she flatter people. Instead, she tried to bring out the good in others, without denying their defects, 'Her tact matched her charity; likewise her leniency did not prevent her from being firm when it was necessary.'[6] That this was the result of spiritual effort is seen in a telling *Diary* entry, 'How hard it is to bear with people's characters!'[7]

Nonetheless, Elizabeth observed the greatest commandments which contain all the virtues: love of God and neighbour. Elizabeth's friendships endured throughout her life, and beyond.

Contemplative in the Midst of the World

Mme Catez loved travelling and the trio spent the summer months touring Switzerland, the South of France, Biarritz, Lourdes, the Pyrenees, Vosges and the Jura. Between the ages of fourteen and twenty, Elizabeth covered 8,000 km by train, an amazing distance in those days. She loved the wonderful vistas of sea and mountains which, for her, symbolized the infinity of God, 'I am mad about these mountains which I sit and contemplate as I write!'[8] In the summer of 1900, Elizabeth was so enthralled by her first view of the Atlantic Ocean that, quite literally, she could not be dragged away by her mother and Guite, who became quite annoyed with her. In her pilgrim state, she experienced intensely the Christian call to live in, or perhaps between, two worlds, the outer observable and the inner hidden.

Elizabeth was a very balanced person and her deepening spiritual life did not make her a killjoy. Indeed, her independent mind saw no harm in dances, contrary to some of the rigorist Jansenistic preaching recorded in her 1899 mission notes, 'It is a grave sin to give oneself up to feasts unless for a serious reason.'[9] Elizabeth reminds us of St Teresa's famous maxim, 'God deliver us from sullen saints!'

Elizabeth entered generously into the continuous round of parties and dances devised by her mother to distract her from Carmel. She was very attractive with a real sparkle in her eye and everyone appreciated her charming personality. A young woman with 'rhythm in her head', she was both a graceful dancer and excellent accompanist and the popular Catez sisters were often called on to play their entertaining piano duets. Notwithstanding her involvement in the social whirl, Elizabeth lived a remarkable interior life:

> Since I cannot break with the world and live in solitude, at least give me solitude of heart, that I may live in such intimate union

with You, that nothing can distract me ... You know well, my Divine Master, that when I mix with the world I find my consolation in recollecting myself in order to enjoy Your presence which I feel so strongly within! No one thinks of You during these gatherings, and it seems to me that You are happy if only one heart, even a poor one like mine, remembers You.[10]

Not only did Elizabeth enjoy a sense of God's presence, she was also aware of bringing that presence with her wherever she was and something of this communicated itself. At one party, a friend overheard the young men discussing potential dancing partners. When they came to Elizabeth they hesitated, 'She is not for us, look at that expression!'[11] During another party, a friend, marvelling at her gaze, asked what she was thinking about. Elizabeth responded spontaneously that she was thinking of 'Him'. People contrasted her increasingly 'luminous gaze' with the angry eyes of the truculent young woman of earlier years.

Elizabeth's sense of the presence of God had another interesting aspect. Once, as a young girl, when walking past a theatre, she exclaimed, 'Oh, I'd love to be an actress!' When her companion expressed surprise, Elizabeth's response was enlightening: 'Yes,' she said, 'because then there would be at least one person there who loved God!'[12]

Everyday Mysticism

Elizabeth's growing spiritual maturity is evident in the way she threw herself into all aspects of her life with an heroic generosity that gave no indication of the cost of the delay in entering Carmel. She lived an everyday mysticism which makes holiness possible for everyone through complete abandonment to the present moment. She walked the humble and ordinary path of holiness. A priest who guided her said:

This pure soul displayed itself before me in all its ardour and innocence ... A restrained enthusiasm gave feeling to a piety that was simple, orderly, and perfectly natural in its supernatural character; there was no exaggeration or craving for what was unusual. The *self* that is so detestable never seemed to have been born in her.[13]

In an age of the ego, where people crave superficial beauty and transitory fame, Elizabeth shows that true, enduring beauty lies in our life with God, 'If you could see the beauty of a soul in the state of grace, you would die of love for it.'[14]

Elizabeth's Parish Apostolate

Elizabeth participated in the parish life of St Michael's with great energy and generosity. She sang in the choir and prepared children for First Communion, having a special way with the more difficult ones who were, as a result, often entrusted to her. She visited the sick workers from the tobacco factory and organized a holiday camp for their children, inventing for them a novel invocation to Mary, 'Our Lady of Tobacco, pray for us.' One of the youngsters, Anne Marie Avout, recalled Elizabeth's vivid imagination and wonderful stories which fascinated them. She was full of fun and often took them for walks, and she was so popular that they used to cling to her skirt and fight over who would link arms with her. 'We absolutely loved her.' In fact, she had to hide her address from them in order to have some peace.[15]

Longing to Enter Carmel

The balcony of Elizabeth's bedroom overlooked the Dijon Carmel and when she heard the monastery bells calling the sisters to prayer, her *Diary* records how she united herself with them. Elizabeth's desire to enter Carmel never wavered; in fact, it intensified, causing her great interior suffering:

> It was a real trial to be taken during the holidays far from my Carmel, from Dijon and its churches that I loved so well. Fond as I was of my friends, I felt a void while in their company; and though I appeared to live, yet I felt lifeless.[16]

A rare, if indirect, insight into how Elizabeth may have coped during this difficult period can be gleaned from the eight letters which she later wrote from Carmel to Germaine de Gemeaux, who also wanted to be a Carmelite, and whose mother, like Elizabeth's, opposed her vocation. These letters are filled with encouragement, reassuring Germaine, as she had probably reassured herself, 'You can be a Carmelite already, for Jesus recognizes the Carmelite from within, by her soul.'[17]

When Elizabeth's confessor, Abbé Sellenet, was leaving Dijon, in 1897, he urged her mother not to oppose her daughter's vocation any longer. Sadly, his words had the opposite effect on Mme Catez who had hoped that Elizabeth had forgotten about Carmel. She panicked and forbade Elizabeth to visit Carmel. Elizabeth obeyed. Deprived even of this consolation, Elizabeth was plunged more deeply into the desert, where she experienced the acute aloneness of which John of the Cross sings, 'With no other light or guide / Than the one that burned in my heart'.[18]

Purity of Heart – 'to will one thing'[19]

Despite her turmoil, Elizabeth's submission to her mother was total: she abandoned attempts at fasting, and even desisted from going to Holy Communion to assuage her mother's displeasure.

Unintentionally, Mme Catez contributed immeasurably to her daughter's spiritual growth. Deprived of external mortifications, Elizabeth turned to the interior mortification of her will, which she resolved to exercise at every possible opportunity, convinced that 'obedience is better than sacrifice'.[20]

> Whatever happens to you, accept it,
> and in the uncertainties of your humble state, be patient,
> since gold is tested by fire
> and chosen men in the furnace of humiliation.[21]

Elizabeth lived Christ's words, 'My food is to do the will of the One who sent me.'[22] She was learning the most important lesson of all: giving up her own will in order to do what God wills. Later, in letters from Carmel, Elizabeth made it clear that she would not have considered entering without her mother's 'Fiat'.[23]

Guite (left) and Elizabeth

Prayer and Self-Knowledge

Unable to live silence and prayer within Carmel, Elizabeth made her life a continual prayer in the 'cell of her heart'. She lived prayer as presence and relationship, the gateway to eternity, and the witness of her interior life is one of her most powerful messages. Prayer strengthened her to work on her over-sensitive, impulsive temperament until she gradually gained self-mastery in the most practical and observable ways. She knew that prayer, as C. S. Lewis recognized, doesn't change God, it changes us.

Elizabeth enjoyed a healthy self-knowledge and devised an effective strategy to prevent herself being 'carried away':

> I was very good-humoured by nature and loved enjoying myself; but even at a young age, I had a fear of worldly amusements lest they should win my heart. However, my resolve to give myself totally to God, preserved me from being carried away by pleasure ... When I was invited to social gatherings, before starting out I used to shut myself in my room and pray for a while, for, knowing my ardent nature, I watched myself carefully.[24]

Elizabeth, wary of the pitfalls of her temperament, planned her day. She anticipated temptations, preparing herself through reflection and prayer; in scriptural terms, she 'put God's armour on'.[25] Both the motivation for and degree of her recollection are significant, her yearning for the Eucharist, which she would receive at Mass the following day.

'Redeemed from fire by fire'

Elizabeth confided her ongoing struggles to her *Diary*:

> It seems to me that whenever I receive an unjust remark, my nature so rebels against it that the blood seems to boil in my veins ... Today I have had the joy of offering my Jesus several sacrifices connected with my dominant fault, but how much they cost me! It proves how weak I am, yet Jesus was with me; I heard His voice in the depths of my heart and then I was ready to endure everything for love of Him![26]

Only her love for Jesus gave her the strength to combat her explosive nature. She fought passion with passion and self-love was replaced by a stronger love of God; she was 'redeemed from fire by fire'.[27] We have to replace the weakness or fault with something else, we cannot remain empty, or like the man in the Gospel, many demons will rush in. Our struggles and desires are what please God and our successes are a bonus. God rewarded Elizabeth's efforts and she eventually gained such self-control that her mother, who had despaired of her daughter's childhood tantrums, was now equally frustrated by Elizabeth's newfound composure, 'Can't you get cross? You drive me mad with your calmness!'[28] Perhaps she intuited the source of Elizabeth's serenity, which recalls the inner tranquillity recommended by the Desert Fathers, and only achieved through radically dying to self and focusing totally on Jesus.

Madame Catez's Illness – Elizabeth's Torment

Mme Catez had never really recovered from the poisonous snakebite and in December 1898, the wound erupted, making her seriously ill. There was a strong possibility that she might either die or become a permanent invalid and Elizabeth had to face the prospect of remaining at home to nurse her mother and never fulfil her dream of entering Carmel. She confided her anxiety to a close friend Marie-Louise Maurel, and poured out her 'torment' in several poems. By the beginning of February 1899, the feast of the Purification, she was resigned to this possibility as a rather poignant *Diary* entry records:

> Since Jesus does not want me yet, His will be done; but may I sanctify myself in the world; may this world not hinder me from going to Him; may I not be taken up, and kept back with futilities! I am the bride of Christ ... May I be ever worthy of Him! May I not waste His graces; and may I have the happiness of proving to Him how much I love Him![29]

Elizabeth's passionate resolve to do God's will is profoundly impressive, and we are moved by such generosity, knowing what it cost her.

Permission to enter Carmel, but not yet ...

Mme Catez slowly recovered her health and on Palm Sunday, during a parish mission in Dijon, she consulted the preacher about Elizabeth's vocation. Guite pleaded with her mother to give Elizabeth permission to follow her vocation and finally, Mme Catez, with many tears, gave her consent (often reconsidered) for Elizabeth to enter Carmel, but not until she was twenty-one. The ban on visiting Carmel was lifted and Elizabeth, overjoyed, wrote in her *Diary* that she was speechless, then enthusiastically composed a twenty-nine stanza poem, a dialogue of love, which was barely legible and whose only title was the momentous date, '26 March 1899'.

To Elizabeth's dismay, only five days later, on Good Friday, Mme Catez returned home, enthusing about a wonderful offer of marriage. Elizabeth could only refuse the proposal as her heart was no longer her own because it belonged totally to Jesus. She unequivocally reaffirmed her vocation in a poem to her 'Crucified Love' and a *Diary* entry, written as a dialogue between Christ and herself. Elizabeth frequently meditated on Jesus in the Garden of Gethsemane inspired, perhaps, by the large paintings of Gethsemane in the public chapel of the Dijon Carmel, which was dedicated to the Agonizing Heart of Jesus and the Transpierced Heart of Mary.

Mme Catez's contradictory behaviour persisted throughout the two-year delay and Elizabeth's *Diary*, 1899–1900, recorded the suffering she endured, 'haunted by this Carmel, which attracts me so'.[30] Unfortunately, prior to entering Carmel, she destroyed the pages written at this time. If Guite had not discovered her in the act of burning her *Diary* and persuaded Elizabeth to entrust the two remaining notebooks to her, they would have been lost to us forever.

Homesick for Carmel and Heaven

One profound effect of this desert period was Elizabeth's increased desire for heaven, which transcended even her longing for Carmel. In a letter to Canon Angles, written only two months before entering, Elizabeth expressed her intense 'homesickness for heaven' and her desire to die even before entering the Dijon Carmel, 'because the Carmel in Heaven is much better, so I'll be a Carmelite just the same in Paradise.'[31] The intense nostalgia for heaven which Augustine called 'restlessness', might explain why she, like many saints, died young. Years earlier, Elizabeth had made a pilgrimage to Notre-Dame d'Etang expressly to ask for the grace to die young, until a distressed Guite found out and stopped her.[32] Elizabeth's prayer, however, was to be answered. Her period of exile had accomplished its work of purification and, paradoxically, Elizabeth entered Carmel when she no longer needed to. She realized that even in Carmel, she was in exile, for this is the human condition. As Chesterton reflected, it is why even at home we feel homesick.[33] It is the vast-triangled ache felt even in the soundest of vocations, the best of marriages, and most fulfilled of lives.

'Suffering from making others suffer'

The last months were very painful for the trio; Elizabeth 'suffered from making others suffer'. Of her mother and sister, she wrote, 'My poor darlings whom I am crucifying.'[34] On the eve of her entrance to Carmel, a friend remarked what a great sacrifice it would be to give up playing the piano but Elizabeth responded that the hardest sacrifice of all was to leave her mother and sister.

Seeing how the delay was affecting Elizabeth's health, Mme Catez went to Carmel immediately after Elizabeth's twenty-first birthday to arrange for her to enter soon. Elizabeth was destined for the new foundation in Paray-le-Monial, but Mme Catez and Guite were worried and wrote to Mother Marie of Jesus about the negative effect it might have on Elizabeth's health. The Prioress responded graciously, 'I see in all this the will of the good God which we should love and do without a second thought. So I shall receive her for Dijon.'[35] Only after the reprieve did Elizabeth admit to Guite how hard it would have been not to enter Dijon. By her holiness, Elizabeth has made the Dijon Carmel famous, associated as it is with her name, the significance of which was first explained to her there.

On the night before entering Carmel, the eve of the First Friday of the month, Elizabeth spent part of the night in prayer. Her mother, unable to sleep, joined her beloved daughter and they wept together, sharing their grief. The next morning, 2 August 1901, Elizabeth knelt down one last time before her father's portrait, to ask his blessing, then set off for Carmel accompanied by her mother, Guite and some friends. There they attended Mass, said their goodbyes and Elizabeth finally stepped over the threshold of Carmel.

The 'beauty of holiness'[36]

Cardinal Newman urged Christians to recognize the 'beauty of holiness'. Elizabeth's self-conquest was noticed by others who marvelled at her calm expression. Her spiritual director had recommended that young Elizabeth do things for God, 'without making a face'. Later, in Carmel, she would be noted for her availability in community, 'there was never the least sign, in her expression, of impatience or surprise.'[37] There is an undeniable congruence between her interior growth and her calm appearance. An entry in the *Diary* of Etty Hillesum, the Dutch Jewish mystic, could have been written about Elizabeth, 'I don't know what it is but something in you has changed ... The countenance of your face, your expressions, they are as lively and expressive as ever, but now there's so much more wisdom behind them.'[38]

Photographs taken at different times, clearly reveal Elizabeth's inner journey and complement the two 'word portraits' in her *Prayer to the Trinity* and *Praise of Glory*. Elizabeth's face gradually became 'radiant with meaning, full of such goodness as can only come from years of cultivating a loving heart'.[39] This contrasts dramatically with the fictional character Dorian Gray, through whom Oscar Wilde explores the idea of an innocent face concealing a hideous soul whose true repulsive visage is manifested only in death. Christ is our truest self-portrait and his was the image that Elizabeth reflected to others.

'The goal is the same'

Nicholl says, 'we know precisely as much as we have suffered, neither more nor less.'[40] Elizabeth amply demonstrates that 'nothing is lost on a journey on which nothing happens in vain.'[41] In the desert Elizabeth recognized that contemplation and action are simply different ways of giving one's life to God in whatever way he wants. The 'one thing necessary' is the deep union of wills. It is not where we are but the direction in which we are travelling that matters. To a friend getting married, she wrote, 'He has chosen two different ways for us, but the goal is the same. Oh, let us be all His, let us truly love Him.'[42]

Notes

1. See *GOS* 41.
2. *Rule of St Benedict*, ch. 58.
3. *Reminiscences*, p. 18.
4. Extern sisters live as Carmelites not bound by enclosure. They act as a link between the enclosed nuns and the outside world.
5. Moorcroft, *My Heaven*, p. 43.
6. *Reminiscences*, p. 18.
7. Ibid., p. 33.
8. *L* 14.
9. *D* 68.
10. *Reminiscences*, p. 42.
11. Moorcroft, *My Heaven*, p. 48.
12. *Reminiscences*, p. 17.
13. Ibid., p. 10.
14. Ibid.
15. Dijon Carmel, *Amour Excessif*, DVD.
16. *Reminiscences*, p. 48.
17. *L* 133.
18. *The Dark Night*, st. 3.
19. Kierkegaard, *Purity of Heart*, title.
20. 1 Sam. 15:22.
21. Sir. 2:4–5, see *GOS* 37.
22. *L* 170.
23. Cf. *L* 94, *L* 97.
24. *Reminiscences*, p. 15.
25. Eph. 6:11.
26. *D* 1.
27. Eliot, 'Little Gidding', *Four Quartets*, l. 206.

28. Dijon Carmel, *Amour Excessif,* DVD.
29. *Reminiscences,* p. 23.
30. *L* 178.
31. *L* 55, see *L* 62.
32. *Reminiscences,* p. 18.
33. Chesterton, *Orthodoxy*, p. 79.
34. *L* 71.
35. *Reminiscences,* p. 63.
36. Newman, *Sermons* VII, p. 34.
37. *EDC*, p. 8.
38. Hillesum, *An Interrupted Life*, p. 106.
39. Nicholl, *Holiness,* p. 49, see p. 140.
40. Ibid., p. 131, see *L* 258.
41. Squire, *Asking the Fathers,* p. 171.
42. *L* 36, see *L* 25, *LG* 32, 38–9.

Elizabeth as a postulant, age 21, with Mother Germaine

Chapter 3

Elizabeth in Carmel

The place God calls you to is the place where
Your deep gladness and the world's deep hunger meet.

Frederick Buechner

Dijon Carmel

The Carmel of Dijon, founded on 21 September 1605, was the third foundation in France after Paris and Pontoise. The holy Spanish Carmelite, Mother Anne of Jesus, a pillar of St Teresa of Avila's reform and one of her most trusted daughters, became prioress of the first French monastery of Discalced Carmelites in Paris and later of the Dijon Carmel, her third foundation, which she praised in the highest terms, 'Whoever seeks for perfection, will find it in the daughters of Dijon.'

Postulant 'inside the walls'

Elizabeth Catez entered Carmel on 2 August 1901, two weeks after her twenty-first birthday, becoming Sr Marie Elizabeth of the Trinity. The fervent Dijon community immediately recognized Elizabeth's virtue. One sister's letter to the Lisieux Carmel proved prophetic, 'Our postulant of three days will become a saint for she already has a remarkable disposition for it.'[1]

The sister serving the meals the week Elizabeth entered noticed how recollected she was in the refectory. Unlike other newcomers, whose eyes were usually everywhere, Elizabeth never looked up. The server thought it 'too good to last; no one could be that mortified on the very first day!'[2] Another sister, Aimée of Jesus, was also sceptical about the genuineness of Elizabeth's goodness. However, after deliberately observing her for some months, she admitted that she had not noticed the least fault. On the contrary, while Elizabeth had her share of weaknesses, she was always humble and never seemed to give in to herself. A Carmelite 'devil's advocate' thus confirmed Elizabeth's integrity, for the sure sign of authentic prayer is its tangible results in one's everyday life.

Although Elizabeth was virtuous, she still had a lot to learn in order to adapt to the rigours of monastic discipline and the asceticism of community living, gradually learning what it means to be a Carmelite in reality as well as name, through a continual process of daily call and response. Notwithstanding her spiritual progress before entering, Elizabeth still had to work on herself, as holiness is an ongoing task.

'My joy increases every day'

Oblivious to the impact she was making on the community, Elizabeth was incredibly happy and wrote enthusiastic letters home, sharing her delight in all the daily details of Carmel. She wrote about everything: her cell, the straw mattress she nearly fell off during the night, the choir, her appetite, even the laundry! The pain of her exile was rewarded initially by great consolation. She created a vivid picture for her dear Canon Angles:

> How good the good God is! I cannot express my happiness, which I realize better every day. There is nothing here but Him; He is all; He suffices and we live by Him alone. I like the hour of the *great silence* best – the time at which I am now writing to you. Picture me to yourself in the little cell of which I am so fond – the tiny sanctuary kept for Him and me alone. You can imagine what happy hours I spend here with Him I love . . . I do not regret the years I spent waiting: such great happiness had to be paid for.[3]

Many elements of Elizabeth's Carmelite spirituality appear in this extract, written only six weeks after she entered: joy in her vocation; total absorption in 'Him' in all circumstances; great love of her Carmelite cell, as the privileged place of encounter with the good God. When we recall the intense suffering Elizabeth endured during her long years of waiting, her final words alone convey her tremendous love and they remind us of Jacob who worked for seven years in order to marry Rachel, and then seven more, 'and they seemed to him like a few days because he loved her so much.'[4]

The sisters were equally impressed with their new postulant and she was received for clothing after only four months (postulancy usually lasts six months). To her great joy, Elizabeth received the Carmelite habit on the feast of the Immaculate Conception, 8 December 1901.

Inner Darkness

After a very happy postulancy, Elizabeth was unexpectedly plunged into darkness during her noviciate, although only Mother Germaine, who was both her prioress and novice mistress, and Sr Marie of the Trinity, her assistant, knew of her inner struggles. Before entering, Elizabeth had experienced a less intense period of darkness when she suffered from the apparent absence of God, which she described as feeling like a wall. Classically, these experiences of God's withdrawal are termed the 'dark night of the senses', the *via negativa*, explained by St John of the Cross. He speaks for all the great mystics, who know from experience that this night, this darkness, is our greatest teacher.

Soon after receiving the habit and beginning the noviciate Elizabeth's health suffered and her dominant fault, hypersensitivity, resurfaced. One can only imagine her distress after all the efforts she had made to overcome herself. It must have felt as if she had lost control, which in itself is an acute form of suffering. The causes are not recorded. While Elizabeth knew she would experience pain in being detached from all that was dear to her, especially the separation from her beloved mother and sister, she could not have anticipated how intensely she would feel the deprivation of that part of her which had been absorbed and expressed through her music. At this point, Carmel must have felt like a death to her very gifted nature and she would also have been affected by the rigorous Carmelite austerity. During that first severe winter, the unheated monastery left her hands so cold that she could barely write and, if you look closely, in one of her profession photos you can see her bandaged fingers, caused by chilblains.

Silent Suffering

Mother Germaine hints at what Elizabeth suffered without giving details. Elizabeth's prayer became dry and she experienced spiritual darkness and scruples, depression, anxieties, and imaginative fantasies which contrasted with anything she had known before. In Elizabeth's *Death Circular,* Mother Germaine tactfully used terms such as 'disquietudes of soul' and 'spiritual anguish', thereby respecting Elizabeth's privacy, reminding contemporary readers that earlier hagiographers often omitted details of human fragility. At a deeper level, however, 'There are secrets which, it would appear, God himself often guards'; and moments over which he draws 'an almost impenetrable veil.'[5] Elizabeth had lost everything she cherished and nothing replaced it but scruples and darkness.

How did Elizabeth cope with this interior struggle, living as she did in community and meeting family and friends in the parlour? The answer is, with impressive fortitude, patience and constancy, which showed the extent of her virtue. She lived by faith and loved without feeling, remaining recollected despite the inner turmoil, preserving such an exterior calm that no one suspected what she was going through. Elizabeth never complained or spoke of her difficulties, either in conversation or letters. Perhaps we get a glimpse of how she coped in the advice she gave to the suffering Mme de Sourdon whom she encouraged to trust that God's 'whole desire is to lead you ever deeper into Himself. Surrender yourself and all your preoccupations to Him.'[6]

Elizabeth persevered through her sufferings sustained by her ardent love for Christ. Her interior trials deepened that self-knowledge which is the foundation of true humility. Elizabeth held on, 'clinging to God through everything', just as she advised others to do, trusting that God was hollowing her out in order to make space for deeper interior blessings. Loving God when there seems to be no return is the mark of a true lover. Prior to entering, Elizabeth had been a very holy young woman. In Carmel she learned to be a holy nun, 'to love Him with all [her] soul, but with a love that is true, strong and generous!'[7]

'To be the Bride of Christ'[8]

While Elizabeth was enduring much mental and spiritual suffering, Guite was overjoyed about her forthcoming marriage to Georges Chevignard. Inspired by the prospect, Elizabeth reflected on her own vocation and wrote a beautiful meditation, 'To be the Bride of Christ', extolling her fiancé's attributes in the spousal language favoured by scripture and mystic. The topic and tone of this profound meditation are even more remarkable given the difficulties she was enduring and it powerfully affirmed Elizabeth's love of God and her unselfish love of Guite whose happiness she shared on her wedding day, on the feast of St Teresa of Avila, 15 October 1902.

'Everything is beginning'

As religious profession approached, Mother Germaine was so concerned about Elizabeth's anguished spiritual state that, on the very eve of her profession, she consulted a priest who reassured them both. Thus, on Sunday morning 11 January 1903, the feast of the Epiphany that year, Sr Elizabeth of the Trinity, aged twenty-two and a half, made her profession. According to the custom at that time, Elizabeth vowed chastity, poverty and obedience forever before the chapter room altar, in the presence of the community.[9] The rest of the day was spent in silence, prayer and thanksgiving, before celebrating with her sisters during the evening recreation. On 21 January 1903, feast of St Agnes, virgin and martyr, Sr Elizabeth received the black veil, in a public ceremony. She wrote to Canon Angles:

> During the night that preceded the great day, while I was in choir
> awaiting the Bridegroom, I understood that my heaven was

beginning on earth: heaven in faith, with suffering and immola-
tion for Him whom I love! I want to love Him so much, to love
Him as my seraphic Mother Teresa did, even unto death. [10]

After an emotionally and spiritually gruelling noviciate, Elizabeth's profession restored her peace, filling her with deep joy.
God had tried Elizabeth, 'as gold is tested by fire' and she had
proved faithful and generous:

> A life of love is so 'easy' in Carmel! . . . How I love the *Rule* which
> shows me the way in which He wishes me to become holy. I do
> not know whether I shall have the joy of giving my Bridegroom
> the testimony of blood, but if I follow the Carmelite observance
> fully, I shall at last have the satisfaction of *spending* myself for
> Him, and for Him alone. [11]

After profession Elizabeth was made assistant in the robe room,
making and mending habits, and assistant at the turn, answering
the bells. She also helped in the noviciate acting as angel to two
postulants. Elizabeth's continued joy in Carmel permeated all her
letters. 'My Carmelite vocation ... moves me to adoration and
thanksgiving . . . I am happy, and it does me good to say so . . . if
you knew how my heart expands, in its contact with the God who
is all Love'. [12]

Gift of Scripture

Until this point, Elizabeth had, of course, always read Scripture.
After profession, however, through reading the 'magnificent
epistles' of St Paul, she received a special 'Gift of Scripture'. The
Word of God, savoured in prayer, spoke to her pure heart nour-
ishing her in St Paul's solid teaching and doctrine. She loved his
writings, recommending him enthusiastically to everyone. St Paul
became her spiritual guide and was to have untold influence on
her, as we shall see. She gives us wonderful insights into Paul's
letters.

Political and Ecclesial Conflict

It is a common misconception that, in the seclusion of enclosure, Carmelites escape the world's problems. One might think it was easy for Elizabeth to make rapid spiritual progress, tucked away in her peaceful French Carmel. In fact, her spiritual calibre can only be fully appreciated against the background of increasing political, ecclesial and diocesan disorder.

At the time Elizabeth entered Carmel, France was in ferment as the government aggressively pursued an antireligious line, systematically tearing State and Church apart. Between 1902 and 1905 nearly two hundred teaching and preaching orders were suppressed, and their buildings and goods were summarily confiscated, leading to the closure of over 3,000 schools and forcing religious and priests to flee the country. On 9 December 1905, a law was passed separating the Church and State, effectively abrogating the 1801 Concordat between Napoleon and Pius VII. Despite Pius X's repeated appeals to the French government and people for the esteemed 'elder daughter' of the Church, *laïcité* took root, making France one of the most secular countries in Catholic Europe.

Diocesan Tumult

The republican sympathies of Monsignor le Nordez, Bishop of Dijon, were the proximate cause of the rupture in diplomatic relations between France and the Vatican. His stance caused an uproar in Dijon and, in February 1904, seminarians refused to be ordained by him and when he dismissed some, others went on strike, only capitulating when threatened with forced enlistment. On 13 June, many parents refused to send their children to the Saint-Benigne Cathedral for Confirmation. Pius X hastily summoned Nordez to Rome and he resigned as Bishop in early September 1904. As a friend of the Catez family, Nordez had presided at Elizabeth's clothing but the Dijon Carmel deliberately arranged Elizabeth's black veiling when he would be away from Dijon, as they also disagreed with his position.

Threat of Expulsion

Despite the Carmelite Order celebrating 300 years in France on 13 June 1904, no festivities are recorded in the Archives of the Dijon Carmel or, indeed, of the Order in France. Perhaps the fraught political and diocesan situations overshadowed this landmark centenary, rendering celebrations inappropriate, possibly even dangerous. The anxiety was historically grounded, as little more than a hundred years earlier on 17 July 1794, during the last days of the Reign of Terror, sixteen Carmelites of Compiègne had been guillotined. The Dijon Carmel held a triduum in honour of the beatification of these Martyrs from 13–15 October 1905.

Conscious of the ever-present threat of persecution and possible expulsion, Mother Germaine visited Switzerland and Belgium in 1903, to secure accommodation should 'her little band' have to escape. However, despite the national and diocesan turbulence, Mother Germaine maintained order and prayerfulness in the monastery.

'Daughter of the Church'

Elizabeth's understanding of her vocation as a true daughter of Teresa of Avila was to be an apostle who was so united with Jesus, that his prayer, in her, poured itself out over the diocese, the Church and the world. Only against this tumultuous background can we comprehend what might otherwise seem to be pious statements, 'My soul loves to unite itself to yours in one and the same prayer for the Church, for the diocese ... we really need God to work resurrections in our dear France.'[13] 'How we feel the need to be sanctified, to forget ourselves in order to belong wholly to the interests of the Church ... Poor France! I love to cover her with the blood of the Just One.'[14]

Aware that the future was dark, Elizabeth rejoiced in having been called to Carmel at this time of persecution, with the possibility of giving her testimony of blood for the sake of Christ and his Church. As she lay dying, Elizabeth encouraged her mother to rejoice in her daughter's participation in Christ's suffering:

Your mother's heart should leap for divine joy in thinking that the Master has deigned to choose your daughter, the fruit of your womb, to associate her with His great work of redemption; that He has signed her with the seal of the cross and that He suffers in her, as it were, an extension of His passion ... He wants me to be another humanity for Him in which He can suffer still more for the glory of His Father, to help the needs of the Church; this thought has done me so much good![15]

This is no mere rhetoric but reality; it is the Christian vocation. Her mother must have experienced a mixture of wonder, distress and pride upon reading her daughter's heroic words.

'Mystery and whole vocation in my name'

It was in this context of unbelievable political and ecclesial disorder that Elizabeth embarked on a silent inner journey of discovery, which began when she entered Carmel and received the name Sr Elizabeth of the Trinity. She had hoped to be called Sr Elizabeth of Jesus, so her name was, initially, a disappointment to her. However, in accepting this name with characteristic generosity, she entered into its depths and it quickly became absolutely central to her spirituality. On the first feast of the Trinity in Carmel, she wrote:

Oh yes, my Guite, this feast of the Three is really my own, for me there is no other like it. It was really lovely in Carmel for it is a feast of silence and adoration: I never understood so well the Mystery and the whole vocation in my name.[16]

In the midst of external chaos, Elizabeth silently entered within, cultivating a life 'hidden with Christ in God',[17] immersing herself in the tranquil Trinity. She was in, but not of, her time and context. We live in noisy, dangerous, troubled times, but so did Elizabeth, even more so. Her gift is to show us a better way; she proves that we can be different, from within: our faith offers us hope-filled possibilities and we need to tell each other the good news.

'Praise of his glory'

Elizabeth's spiritual life developed further, through her 'beloved
St Paul'. While reading Ephesians 1, she received the grace of her
personal vocation when she discovered her new name, 'Praise of
Glory'. Many themes merge in this outpouring of her spirit: her
desire to live in union with the Trinity, in order to be holy and an
apostle of love in the Church, thus becoming the 'Praise of Glory
of the Trinity'. She shared her discovery with Canon Angles:

> I am going to tell you a very personal secret: my dream is to be 'the
> praise of his glory'. I read that in St Paul and my bridegroom made
> me understand that this was to be my vocation while in exile,
> waiting to sing the eternal Sanctus in the City of the saints.[18]

As her health declined, Elizabeth's spirit soared, delighting in St
Paul's writings and relishing the wonder of being *Laudem Gloriae*.
As early as 1903 Elizabeth had been diagnosed with Addison's
disease, which at that time was incurable. The symptoms were
painful and distressing: loss of appetite and weight, exhaustion,
severe headaches, insomnia, stomach disorders and finally death.
Perhaps the 'new name,' as so often in Scripture, indicated a
change of direction, in this instance, towards Calvary.

The Road to Calvary

Lent 1905 was a terrible struggle as Elizabeth felt exhausted all
the time. Each evening, overcome by weakness, she struggled
back to her cell, holding on to the wall for support. By August
1905, she was relieved of her duties, in the hope that time spent
resting in the garden, in the fresh air might restore her. Despite
their best efforts, however, Elizabeth's health deteriorated
rapidly and in Lent 1906, she was moved permanently to the
infirmary. Only there did her sisters begin to recognize the extent
of her recollection and holiness. On Palm Sunday 8 April, they
thought she was dying and she received the Last Sacraments. A
serious relapse occurred on Good Friday 13 April, followed by an
unexpected improvement on Holy Saturday.

No one had dared to tell her mother how ill Elizabeth was, but

Mother Germaine broke the news to Mme Catez on Monday of Holy Week. Despite the terrible blow, and Elizabeth's being too weak to come to the parlour, her mother wrote a wonderfully consoling letter which revealed how far she had come in her union with God and acceptance of his will. Elizabeth cherished this comforting letter, reading it again and again. From that time on, Elizabeth expected to die at any moment and she wrote beautiful letters to her mother and Guite, full of spiritual advice, comfort and love.

The Dijon community found it impossible to describe adequately the excruciating suffering Elizabeth endured in the last eight months of her life. Her tongue became so ulcerated and inflamed that she could hardly eat or drink and she literally became 'a living flame of love' as her body wasted away. Sometimes she could hardly speak because of the internal inflammation. Once she whispered, her face radiant, 'Our God is a consuming fire, He is acting upon me.'[19] Her sisters marvelled at her incredible strength and faith. 'My illness seems to me rather mysterious,' she said, 'I call it love's ailment . . . I give myself up and am resigned to it, for I rejoice beforehand in whatever He will do to me.'[20]

From the feast of the Exaltation of the Cross, 14 September onwards, Elizabeth was particularly sustained by Angela de Foligno's words, 'Where then did he dwell, but in suffering?'[21] Mother Marie of Jesus, by then Prioress at Paray-le-Monial, made a last visit to the Dijon Carmel and wrote to her community:

> I have had a beautiful sermon coming in contact with Sr Elizabeth of the Trinity. The little sister is a real saint: she speaks of her approaching death with a lovely simplicity, a joyous serenity and peace, and lives in the anticipation of God, in perfect surrender and love. She seems to be already in the retreat of eternity.[22]

'In the light of eternity'

Elizabeth knew she was dying, so in early August she composed a ten-day retreat, *Heaven in Faith,* as a 'souvenir' for Guite. She then made her own final retreat, her 'noviciate for heaven', *The Last Retreat of Laudem Gloriae.*

Notwithstanding her deepening immersion in God and increasing physical exhaustion, Elizabeth wrote affectionate farewells, advising, encouraging and reassuring friends of her prayers for their various needs: for the safe delivery of a baby (Marie-Louise Morel had lost her first baby the year before); to ease a mother's anxiety over a difficult daughter; even promising to have a word with Our Lady about finding suitable husbands for three friends! Elizabeth also left precious spiritual gifts, 'her faith in God's love', 'her devotion to the Trinity', her 'recipe' for holiness. A final letter to her friend Mme de Bobet, contains the wisdom of a spiritual master, offering a veritable programme for life:

> We see the true value of things in the light of eternity. Oh! How empty is all that has not been done for God and with God! I beg you to mark all you do with the seal of love; it is the only thing that lasts! What a serious thing life is! Each minute is given us for the purpose of rooting ourselves more deeply in God ... The secret of realizing this plan is to forget self ... to look upon the divine Master and on Him alone; to receive joy or sorrow indifferently, as both coming from His love. This establishes the soul on the summits where all is peace.

She goes on to bequeath her friend the best of all gifts:

> I leave you my faith in the presence of God, Who is all love, dwelling within our souls; I entrust it to you.[23]

On 29 October, Elizabeth's family visited for the last time. As they were saying their final goodbye, Elizabeth turned to her beloved mother:

> Mother, when the extern sister comes to tell you that my sufferings are over, you must kneel down and say, 'My God, Thou hast given her to me; I give her back to Thee. Blessed be Thy holy name!'[24]

Madame Catez did exactly as Elizabeth asked. What a transformation of grace in this mother's life and heart.

'To light, to love, and to life'

On 31 October, Elizabeth received the Anointing of the Sick and on the feast of All Saints, 1 November, she received Holy Communion for the last time as she was unable to eat or drink from then on. When her sisters asked for a farewell word, she said, 'At the evening of my life love alone remains . . . All I want now is to live by love.'[25] Her sisters described their distress at beholding her emaciated body and their wonder at her deep recollection:

> I will never forget the impression she made on me those last nine days. On the one hand it was deeply moving to see her poor body, totally unrecognizable, which made one think of Jesus being taken down from the Cross; and on the other hand, I had a profound admiration for her, so utterly was she taken up into the great mystery of the world to come that it was impossible for her to describe what was happening to her.[26]

She seemed to inhabit a very 'thin place', lingering on the very threshold of eternity.

God was working on his loving servant to the very end. At times, 'she felt as if her brain were on fire' and her speech was barely decipherable, but she never lost her dignity. Her 'bloodshot eyes remained closed until the last moments.' She seemed dead, but she lived in God. The words of St Paul, 'I live, no longer I, but Christ lives in me', engraved on her profession crucifix, were etched on her ravaged body and written by her whole life.

Elizabeth died around 6.15 am on 9 November 1906. Her last intelligible words were, 'I am going to light, to love, and to life', which she murmured like a refrain.

'Martyr of love'

It is said that people die as they live. Elizabeth lived as she died: giving herself lovingly, totally, regardless of the cost, to the One whom she loved so deeply:

> A Carmelite is a soul who has gazed on the Crucified. She has seen Him offering Himself to the Father as a Victim; and, reflecting

upon this great vision of the charity of Christ, she has understood
His passionate love and wanted to give herself to Him.[27]

Once God had captured Elizabeth's heart she was irrevocably His
and this loving intimacy, this indwelling, this union, was like a
strong, unbreakable thread running through her life. There was
no change upon entering Carmel, Elizabeth simply continued her
journey into the loving abyss of God's indwelling presence. In
death, God fulfilled her lifetime's desire to be a witness, a
'martyr of love':

'O precious in the eyes of the Lord, is the death of his faithful.'[28]

Notes

1. Moorcroft, *My Heaven*, p. 70.
2. *Reminiscences*, p. 206.
3. *L* 91.
4. Gen. 29:20.
5. Squire, *Asking the Fathers*, p. 228.
6. *L* 129.
7. *L* 38.
8. See *PN* 13, *OC*, p. 904.
9. They did not make temporary vows at that time. The Church has since
   changed this so that everyone has a period of temporary vows.
10. *L* 169.
11. Ibid.
12. *L* 219.
13. *L* 225.
14. *L* 256.
15. *L* 309.
16. *L* 113.
17. Col. 3:3.
18. *L* 256.
19. *Reminiscences*, p. 206.
20. Ibid., p. 150.
21. Ibid., p. 127.
22. Arendup, *The Life of Mother Marie of Jesus*, p. 144.
23. *L* 333.
24. *Reminiscences*, p. 209.
25. Ibid., p. 209.
26. Ibid., p. 217.
27. *L* 133.
28. Ps. 115(116):15, *LOH* I, p. [297].

Part II
Elizabeth's Spirituality

Elizabeth, age 14

Chapter 4

Baptized Living – Called to Holiness

> The Godward journey is a journey on which every individual
> is launched, all unknowingly, at birth.
>
> *Christopher Bryant*

Godward Journey

Life is God's gift to us, what we do with it, is our gift to God.
Viktor Frankl, after three harrowing years in concentration
camps, observed, 'He who has a *why* to live can bear with almost
any *how*.'[1] It is meaning which sustains and vitalizes us. We have
no choice about birth and death, but what happens in between is
all ours. Birth is the beginning of a Godward journey as we belong
to God's family from the first moment of our existence. After
birth, however, we receive the 'second gift', the gift of grace,
through the sacrament of baptism, which is the foundation of the
spiritual journey and offers us the possibility and challenge of a
life of holiness:

> We cannot evade the great and decisive task laid on us by our
> baptism: to become Christians, to accept God by a free decision
> of our innermost being, with our whole heart and mind.[2]

Until the Second Vatican Council, baptism was, in some ways, a
forgotten sacrament and we needed to reclaim and proclaim its
importance. We still urgently need to rediscover its richness if
we are to understand our relationship to ourselves, to God and to
others, in fact, what the Christian life is all about. Augustine
spent all of his energies in the first half of his life on the wrong

things. In one of the most moving spiritual passages ever written,
he captures the anguish of the search and the ecstasy of discovery:

> Late have I loved you, O Beauty so ancient and so new; late have
> I loved you! For behold you were within me, and I outside; and I
> sought you outside and in my ugliness fell upon all those things
> that you have made. You were within me and I was not with you.
> I was kept from you by those things, yet had they not been in you,
> they would not have been at all. You called and cried to me and
> broke open my deafness: and you sent forth your beams and
> shone upon me and chased away my blindness: you breathed
> fragrance upon me, and I drew in my breath and do now pant for
> you: I tasted you, and now hunger and thirst for you: you touched
> me, and I have burned for your peace.[3]

Only when Augustine finally found God did he realize what he
had been missing for so long. Once converted, he sought baptism
and devoted his life completely to God.

'God-shaped vacuum'

Augustine's most famous words resonate throughout our whole
being, 'You have made us for yourself, O Lord, and our hearts are
restless until they rest in you.' He articulates the inner longings
we all experience and which nothing can appease. Through
baptism we do not just need God, we actually become a longing
for God, we experience a 'God-shaped vacuum' in our hearts
which no thing, no achievement, no person or relationship, can
satisfy. All the hungers of our heart are really only one hunger,
the infinite longing, which can only be filled by the Infinite God,
made known to us through Jesus Christ. John of the Cross teaches
that God loves us according to his divine capacity and baptism
gives us an infinite capacity to receive God's love. However, we
are only as great or as small as what we love so, when we set our
desires on anything less than God, our hearts become shrivelled
and God cannot 'fit into an occupied heart'.[4]

Once we deeply absorb these truths, we stop searching in all
the wrong places. We accept longing and restlessness as our
permanent condition this side of the grave and we begin to disen-

gage ourselves from the compulsive behaviours with which we try to fill the emptiness. We embark on the journey to freedom through engaging with the grace of baptism.

Boundless Blessings of Baptism

Baptism elevates human nature to the beauty of God. It contains everything we need as, through grace, we have become 'partakers, sharers in the divine nature'.[5] Baptism makes us people of the beyond, mystics: our horizons are eternal. Luther conveys some of the astonishment we should feel when we reflect on what baptism means:

> In Baptism every Christian has enough to study and to practise all his life. He always has enough to do to believe firmly what Baptism promises and brings – victory over death and the devil, forgiveness of sin, God's grace, the entire Christ, and the Holy Spirit with his gifts. In short, the blessings of Baptism are so boundless that if timid nature considers them, it may well doubt whether they could all be true.[6]

Elizabeth shares this sense of wonder, encouraging us to nourish ourselves on the deep truths of the Christian faith so that our understanding of baptism, like a time-release capsule, dissolves its meaning and grace slowly into our lives. In Elizabeth we see what can happen when we fully respond to the grace of baptism; this is one of her gifts to us. She shows us the possibility of aspiring to a graced, baptismal life. Elizabeth appreciated how blessed she was to have been drawn to God from an early age, 'My God ... thank you from the bottom of my heart for showing me from my youth the vanity of worldly things ... for the graces you have given me!'[7] She felt herself strongly attracted to the depths of things, especially of her own soul. It was a great joy to her to be told that she had not offended God, while Canon Angles, who probably knew her best, believed she died in her baptismal innocence.

'Filled with reverence'

We hear little in Elizabeth's letters about birthdays but she loved
to commemorate the anniversary of her baptism, which she celebrated as the feast of her soul. She had an incredible understanding and appreciation of the significance of baptism. While the
beauty of the newborn disarms us, as we gaze in wonder at the
miracle of life, Elizabeth sees much more deeply, opening our
eyes to the real miracle of grace which occurs in baptism. She
writes to ask Guite the date of Sabeth's baptism, so that she can
accompany her in spirit as the 'Holy Trinity descends into her
soul.'[8] Elizabeth, contemplating the mystery of grace, is 'filled
with reverence before this little temple of the Holy Trinity.'
Echoing Teresa of Avila's famous image, she describes the soul as
a 'crystal which radiates God', before which she would 'kneel
down to adore Him who dwells within her.'[9]

Elizabeth meditated deeply upon the awesome reality that the
soul's deepest truth is that it shares the life of God. She wrote a
wonder-filled letter to her nieces, Sabeth and Odette:

> To those who contemplate you in your mama's arms, you seem
> very small, but your fond aunt who looks on you with the eyes of
> faith sees in you a nature of infinite grandeur, because from all
> eternity you were in the mind of God. He 'intended you to
> become true images of His Son'[10] and, by holy Baptism, He has
> clothed you with Himself, thus making you His children, and at
> the same time His 'living temple'.[11]

> O dear little sanctuaries of love, when I see the splendour that
> radiates in you, and yet which is only the dawn, I fall silent and
> adore Him who creates such marvels![12]

Every Baptized Soul

God has always carried us in his heart. We think life begins when
we are born, on a certain day, in a particular place. In reality,
however, having been in the mind and heart of God from all eternity, we arrive on earth 'trailing clouds of glory'.[13] God has
cherished me from all eternity, that is how important I am. The

true source of my dignity is not wealth, status, fame, posses-
sions. It is the fact that I have been loved into existence by God.
Each of us is a unique, beautifully crafted image of God, called
to grow in his likeness. Teresa of Avila says that we simply
cannot imagine the great beauty and dignity of the baptized
soul.[14] In Elizabeth we see someone who took this utterly seriously, and who knew that her vocation was the call of every
baptized Christian:

> 'One thing alone is necessary: Mary has chosen the better part,
> which shall not be taken from her.' This better part, which seems
> to be my privilege in my beloved solitude of Carmel, is offered by
> God to every baptized soul. He offers it to you ...[15]

Elizabeth offers this robust advice fully aware of the human difficulties of the situation. Her evangelical passion for the holiness of
her friends anticipated the teaching of the Vatican Council in
Lumen Gentium. The heading of Chapter 5 says it all, 'The Univer-
sal Call to Holiness'. 'All Christ's faithful have an invitation,
which is binding, to the pursuit of holiness and perfection in their
own state of life.'[16] Holiness is our deepest calling; it is our
dignity and destiny.

'Only one vocation'

The Carmelite way of life is essentially the Christian way of life,
lived intensely at the very heart of the Church, witnessing to the
goal to which we are all called: union with God in the depths of
our soul. Thomas Merton shared Elizabeth's conviction, 'In practice, there is only one vocation: you are called to interior life
with God, to mystical prayer and to pass on the fruits of contemplation to others.'[17] Through baptism we are mystics in the
making, when we surrender ourselves to the living, loving,
Triune God.

Transformed into Christ

Baptism is both gift and invitation. Even before we respond to
this gift, the reality of it already exists within us. If we do not

respond, we are like a crystal left in darkness. But if we do respond and allow God's radiance to shine in us, we are transformed into light and splendour, becoming a crystal that radiates God. As St Augustine marvelled, God is closer to me than I am to myself. Accepting the invitation of baptism places us in the truth, which makes us free and sets us on a lifelong journey. *Guadium et Spes* puts it starkly: 'Without God every person is an unanswered question.'[18] The answer to that question is the person of Christ:

> In reality, it is only in the mystery of the Word made flesh that the mystery of humanity truly becomes clear . . . Christ is the very revelation of the mystery of the Father and of his love, he fully reveals humanity to itself and brings to life its very high calling.[19]

Reflecting on Jesus as the apex of revelation, John of the Cross asserts that God, after uttering his Word, has no more to say: everything has been given to us in Jesus Christ. Baptism plunges us into the mystery of the life and death of Christ and graces us with the capacity to become Christ, which is the aim of all holiness. In her *Prayer to the Trinity* Elizabeth expresses the profound theological reality of our baptismal grace, praying that she might become 'a kind of incarnation of the Word, another humanity for him in which he can renew his whole mystery.'

The Greatness of our Vocation

Elizabeth wholeheartedly embraces the deep truths of our faith, which we know and believe but tend to take for granted. Her life, therefore, sheds light on these realities so that we see them with fresh eyes and heart. She awakens within us an appreciation of the greatness of our Christian calling and of all that God's grace can accomplish in a responsive heart.

Elizabeth's last letter to Françoise de Sourdon, in which she attempts to answer the many questions posed by her young friend, is a spiritual keepsake, full of practical and challenging advice to all who, despite human fragility, long to live their baptismal calling to the full. A mini treatise on the spiritual life, it has echoes of de Caussade and Francis de Sales, Elizabeth's spiritual forebears, teaching us how to live our Christian baptismal vocation in the ordinary circumstances of everyday life.

Baptized Living

Elizabeth is eminently practical, recommending an everyday mysticism whereby through prayer, faith and love, everything brings us God.[20] The soul is 'truly great, truly free' when it is following God's will. 'Nothing is trivial even when we are performing the most ordinary tasks, because we do not live in these things, we go beyond them.'[21] This faith vision simplifies life, gives us God, and is one of Elizabeth's most encouraging insights, speaking as it does to each one's particular way of life, thereby making holiness accessible to all. We are reminded of Michelangelo's friend who chided him for labouring over trivial parts of a sculpture. The great artist responded that attention to the trivial is what makes perfection and perfection is never trivial. To the visionary, nothing is too small for love, 'Look at every suffering and every joy as coming directly from Him, and then your life will be a continual communion, since everything will be like a sacrament that will give you God.'[22]

We are called to baptized living as opposed to merely existing. We believe that everything accomplished in the name of the Father, Son and Holy Spirit becomes 'baptized'. In baptism, we receive an infinite waterfall of grace which, when we open ourselves to receive it, continually cascades, saturating every area of our lives. We are called to be sacrament, to baptized behaviour, baptized thinking, baptized imagination. Elizabeth invites us to take our baptism seriously; to live the truth of who we really are and to attain 'the ideal life of the soul'. She repeatedly urges us to immerse ourselves in God, so that we partake of the very life of God, the life of the Trinity, gifted to us in baptism. Anything less is unworthy; life is too short, too precious not to lay hold of this gift. The true mystic lives life fully, seeing things as they really are, and cries out to us, in the words of St Leo the Great, 'O Christian, be aware of your nobility.'[23]

Through baptism, we are all called to live supernaturally, by

Elizabeth, age 18

faith. Steeped in St John of the Cross' spirituality Elizabeth asserts that faith gives us God, if we only apprehend. Elizabeth's insistent and timeless message is expressed poetically by T. S. Eliot:

> . . . But to apprehend
> The point of intersection of the timeless
> With time, is an occupation for the saint—
> No occupation either, but something given
> And taken, in a lifetime's death in love,
> Ardour and selflessness and self-surrender.
> For most of us, there is only the unattended
> Moment . . .[24]

Elizabeth, like many saints, is persuasive and inviting when speaking on holiness and, at the same time, rigorous and unrelenting in describing the demands of holiness. She writes, 'dying to self is the law for every Christian . . . it takes on a delightful sweetness when we consider that the aim of this death to self is to replace our life of sins and miseries with the life of God.'[25] This is our baptismal calling: to become other Christs.

Unspiritual vs. Spiritual Living

Evelyn Underhill vividly conveys how diminishing it is to limit oneself to what is unspiritual:

> We mostly spend our lives conjugating three verbs: to Want, to Have, and to Do. Craving, clutching, and fussing on the material, political, social, emotional, intellectual – even on the religious plane – we are kept in perpetual unrest; forgetting that none of these verbs has any significance, except in so far as they are transcended and included in the fundamental verb to be. Being, not wanting, having, and doing, is the essence of a spiritual life.[26]

Elizabeth experiences a 'profound compassion' for those who live for 'nothing higher than this world', as they are slaves, selling themselves short, when they are made for greater things. Her strong and virile spirituality offers an antidote to our agitated, compulsive world and a sound and sure way of faith, which transforms those who follow it. She shows that peace can only come with concern for the spiritual, and she reveals the happiness which flows from a life of prayer and dedication to the things of God.

His Living Temple

Through baptism we each become a dwelling place of God, a living temple. Elizabeth had an unwavering sense of the presence of God within; she felt herself to be a living tabernacle and experienced an unquenchable desire to remain within, keeping company with the indwelling God. The Gospel revelation, 'The kingdom of heaven is within you',[27] so dear to Teresa of Avila, was also a living reality for Elizabeth, who constantly referred to the 'heaven of her soul'. She delighted in the presence of God within and wrote, even before entering Carmel, 'There, in the depths of my heart, in the Heaven of my soul, I love to find Him, since He never leaves me. "God in me, I in Him." Oh, that is my life!'[28] Elizabeth experienced Carmel as an 'anticipated Heaven', and from this privileged place of silence and prayer, she shared one of her most beautiful insights:

I have found my Heaven on earth, since Heaven is God, and God is in my soul. The day I understood this everything became clear to me. I would like to whisper this secret to those I love so they too might always cling to God through everything.[29]

Elizabeth longed to communicate the wonder of this reality so that others might know, love and enjoy the indwelling presence of God, 'Through everything we see Him for we bear Him within us and our life is an anticipated Heaven. I ask God to teach you all these secrets.'[30] Her words urge us to nourish ourselves on these profound realities, in order to discover the amazing life God offers us in the here and now. Confident that her experience is possible for every Christian, she inspires us to open ourselves to the presence of God and his mystery, to live with him in the 'heaven of our soul'. She is passionate about sharing this:

I am asking the Holy Spirit to show you this presence of God within you that I spoke about ... Saint Paul says this, it is enough

to believe: God is spirit and we approach Him through faith.
Realize that your soul is a temple of God ... at every moment of
the day and night the three Divine Persons are living within you
... the Divinity, that essence the blessed adore in heaven, is in
your soul; there is a wholly adorable divine intimacy when you
realize that; you are never alone again![31]

'I so love this mystery of the Holy Trinity'

Elizabeth of the Trinity had an unerring instinct for theological
essentials, since the mystery of the Most Holy Trinity is the
central mystery of Christian faith, the *initium Fidei*.[32] We assent
to this with our heads, but perhaps not always with our hearts and
lives. Rahner said we need to rehabilitate our perceptions because
the rather dry word 'Trinity' seems abstract and intellectual.
Theological descriptions leave our brains muddled and our hearts
cold, whereas, in reality, the Trinity is not a problem to be solved
but a mystery to be lived. The highest stage of prayer and the
goal of every Christian life is mystical contemplation of the
Trinity:

> The whole world round is not enough to fill
> The heart's three corners but it craveth still.
> Only the Trinity who made it can
> Suffice the vast triangled heart of man.[33]

A 'thin place'

The Celtic tradition talks about 'thin places' where, in some indefinable way, the other world feels nearer, the distance between
heaven and earth seems gossamer. Elizabeth herself is a kind of
'thin place'. While, theologically, every Christian is 'of the
Trinity' through baptism, Elizabeth lived this grace to a very high
degree. Her name fascinated her, functioning as a verbal mandala,
and by immersing herself in contemplation, she entered word-
lessly into the inner reality.

Elizabeth repeatedly invites us to believe in, surrender to,
allow this sublime mystery to transform us. She gives us a fresh
and engaging way into this Mystery of Mysteries. She never

defines it, never tries to explain it, she simply marvels and her 'Trinitarian amazement' awakens our longing. Her compelling joy and love for the Trinity attract us, her spark sets us alight. Her palpable intimacy and joy in her 'Three' speak to us as she provides a personal connection with this ineffable mystery. Like Julian of Norwich, Elizabeth almost domesticates God; he is her hearth and home, and she his.

Prayer to the Trinity[34]

Augustine is credited by Aquinas with providing the Church's first major statement of how we can think of God as three in one. Down the ages many saints have extolled the permanent loving exchange of the Trinity. Elizabeth, however, can be credited with enlivening and personalizing this mystery. Her *Prayer to the Trinity*, an act of offering which echoes St Thérèse's *Act of Oblation* and St Catherine of Siena's *Prayer to the Trinity*, both of which she loved, is nonetheless distinctively hers. It is an intimate exchange, between herself and God, which was only found among her notes after she died. Unique in conveying her almost tangible closeness with 'the Three', it encapsulates Elizabeth's whole spiritual journey, beginning and ending in the God who is Trinity. This prayer reveals how she lived and prayed, providing a beautiful inner portrait of a soul in love.

The *Prayer to the Trinity* is much more than a prayer, it is sacramental, because it effects what it signifies. The simplicity, power and conviction of her words open up new horizons of possibility. The prayer transports us into the heart of the eternal love exchange which is Trinity, that '*Mysterium, Tremendum et Fascinans*', 'tremendous and fascinating mystery'.[35] Within that sacred space, she draws us ever more deeply into the abyss wherein we lose ourselves. The unspeakable secrets of God are communicated in ways that transcend words. It is said that when you truly pray, the prayer prays you, and you become what you pray. Elizabeth's prayer supplies a profound way of relating to the indwelling Trinity, the key contemplative experience of the Christian life. The Church implicitly recognizes this in citing Elizabeth's *Prayer to the Trinity* as the culminating expression of the section on the Trinity in the Catechism, indicating that we can only enter into the mystery of the Trinity through prayer.

This prayer, a hymn of profound adoration of a 'Praise of Glory' was accomplished in Elizabeth as she offered herself unreservedly to her 'Three' in total self-gift. In the language of lover and mystic, she wrote in her letters of 'disappearing, losing herself, letting herself be invaded by the Three':[36]

> I should like . . . to lose myself, to be transformed into the Blessed Trinity Who dwells [within]; then my motto, 'my luminous ideal', as you call it, would be realized and I should really be 'Elizabeth *of the Trinity*'.[37]

It seems that God accepted Elizabeth's self-offering, as through her final illness, she became a living *Prayer to the Trinity*.

Icon of the Trinity

The Holy Spirit, the 'divine iconographer', transfigured Elizabeth of the Trinity into an icon of the Trinity. Gazing contemplatively on her, we become partakers of the Trinitarian mystery; as we enter deeply into our God, we in turn, become icons. It took the Church five centuries and four ecumenical councils to express the Trinity theologically. In the short span of Elizabeth's life, the Holy Spirit gifted her with the charism of becoming a unique window onto this mystery of the inner life of God. Pascal said that 'the serene beauty of a holy life is the most powerful influence in the world next to the power of God.' It is, in reality, an expression of the power of God:

> In Elizabeth we see the supernatural life infused at baptism developing normally until she reaches the vision of God, according to the unity of the divine plan. Her life is what God wills every life to be. It begins with the indwelling of the Blessed Trinity to end in the experiential awareness even in this world, whilst we await the revelation in heaven. Such is the simple programme of every Catholic life. Through Elizabeth's life we rejoice in its clear, direct, simple, and rigorously theological development.[38]

Elizabeth knew that life in Christ is a Godward journey from baptism to glory and her life shows what every life could be: through baptism we are not just brought to faith in the Trinity, we are brought *into* the Trinity. At our deepest centre, we are dwelling places of the Triune God, therefore we have both the need and the capacity to enjoy a relationship with this God of love. The aim of our prayer and our life is transformation into this God in whose image we are made: to let ourselves be invaded by him; to lose ourselves in him.

Notes

1. Frankl, *Man's Search for Meaning*, p. vii.
2. Rahner, *On Prayer*, p. 83, see Dt. 6:4–7.
3. *LOH* III, 224*.
4. *LF* 3.48.
5. 2 Pet. 1:4, see *CCC* 1692.
6. Tranvik, 'Luther on Baptism', p. 75.
7. *Reminiscences,* p. 36.
8. *L* 196.
9. *L* 197.
10. See Rom. 8:29.
11. See 2 Cor. 6:16.
12. *L* 240.
13. 'Intimations of Immortality', *Selections from Wordsworth*, p. 128.
14. *IC* I.1. See *LF* 4.14.
15. *L* 129.
16. *LG* 5.42.
17. Merton, *Elected Silence*, p. 371.
18. *GS* 21.
19. *GS* 22, see Bloom, *God and Man*, p. 61.
20. *L* 264.
21. *GV* 8.
22. *L* 264.
23. *LOH* I, p. 187. See *CCC* 1691.
24. Eliot, 'The Dry Salvages', *Four Quartets*, ll. 200ff.
25. *GV* 3.
26. Underhill, *The Spiritual Life*, p. 20.
27. *Way*, ch. 28.
28. *L* 62.
29. *L* 122.
30. *L* 123.
31. *L* 273.
32. *CCC* 234.

33. Underhill, *Mysticism,* p. 135.
34. Given in full at the end of the book, p. 132.
35. Otto, *The Idea of the Holy.*
36. *L* 172.
37. *L* 185.
38. *Reminiscences,* p. 174.

Elizabeth in her First Communion dress

Chapter 5

Eucharistic Amazement

Those of us who are most familiar with the Spirit's promises
are in the greatest danger, familiarity may not breed contempt,
but it takes the edge off awe; promises that drop the jaws or
widen the eyes of newcomers provoke no more than a raised
eyebrow in the old-timers who have ceased to dream.

Jim McGuiggan

'Rekindle Eucharistic amazement'

Baptism and Eucharist are the two great sacraments of encounter
with God. They tell us who we are and provide the grace we need
to fulfil our Christian calling. Baptism establishes us in God and
the Eucharist, 'preserves, increases and renews the life of grace
received at Baptism.'[1] Only in and through the Eucharist do we
get the strength we need to follow Christ and sustain baptized
living; it is 'the source and summit of the Christian life'.[2] Everything is bound up with and directed towards the Eucharist, which
'contains the entire spiritual wealth of the Church: Christ
himself, our Passover and living bread.'[3] During his long pontifi-
cate, John Paul II endeavoured to put the Eucharist back at the
centre of the Church's life, to reawaken our appreciation and love
of this Sacrament of Sacraments 'in all its radiant mystery'. On
Holy Thursday 2003, he promulgated *Ecclesia de Eucharistia*, a
wonderful meditation on the Eucharist, which begins with the
powerful statement, 'The Church draws her life from the
Eucharist'. It is a sustained invitation to 'rekindle Eucharistic
amazement'.[4]

School of the Saints

How do we strengthen our faith and renew our enthusiasm for
the wonderful mystery of the Eucharist, the 'gift beyond description which the Catholic Church has received from Christ'?[5] The
Eucharist played an altogether special role in the lives of saints,
who have much to teach us:

> Let us take our place at the school of the saints, who are the great
> interpreters of Eucharistic piety. In them the theology of the
> Eucharist takes on all the splendour of a lived reality; it becomes
> 'contagious' and, in a manner of speaking, it 'warms our hearts'.[6]

The saints understood the secrets of the Eucharist and manifested
their love in various ways. St Aloysius felt such reverence that he
only received Holy Communion once a week, spending three
days in preparation and three days in thanksgiving. Many saints
kept close to Christ through making frequent visits to Jesus in the
Blessed Sacrament. St Margaret Mary used to take her letters into
Church and read them to her Lord and St Thomas Aquinas often
leaned his head against the tabernacle, in a gesture of great intimacy and affection. St Maximilian Kolbe visited the Blessed
Sacrament at least ten times a day and friends say that is where he
gained the courage to give his life for another in Auschwitz. The
saints were irresistibly drawn to Jesus' presence and, through
contact with this mystery of love, they became that mystery for
others.[7]

Elizabeth of the Trinity is another great 'Saint of the
Eucharist'. From her earliest years, she had a strong sense of the
two foundational sacraments. Each year she honoured her
baptism as the feast of her soul and she treasured her First Holy
Communion as the most beautiful day of her life. A thoroughly
Christian saint, she happily used the ordinary means available to
us all, not seeking anything different or extraordinary. In great
simplicity, she so grounded her life and holiness on the essentials
of faith, that her awareness of their richness and beauty refreshes
our own appreciation of all that we have been given. She particularly helps us to rediscover a sense of awe and wonder at the
greatness of God's loving self-gift in the Eucharist.

Sacrament of Love

The Eucharist is, primarily, the sacrament of God's love. In letters to her priest friend, Abbé Chevignard, Elizabeth pours out her love for the Eucharist in one of her most memorable insights:

> It seems to me that nothing better expresses the love in God's heart than the Eucharist: it is union, consummation, He in us, we in Him, and isn't that Heaven on earth? . . . everything disappears and it seems that one is already entering into the mystery of God! This whole mystery is so much 'ours'.[8]

For Elizabeth, the Eucharist is the supreme expression of God's loving heart, it is *the* sacrament of love in which God reaches out, uniting himself intimately to us. This encounter is composed of ritual, gesture, giving and receiving, but both immediately and ultimately, it defies explanation, transcending words. The inner reality of Eucharist is beyond our understanding and imaginings; it is an encounter with the living God; it is heaven on earth. Eucharist is the closest we attain to God this side of eternity, as our Bishops have reflected, 'In the liturgy of the Church we are drawn into a living communion with Jesus Christ, who reveals to us the love of the Father in the Holy Spirit.'[9] In *Mister God, This is Anna*, the young mystic Anna, reflects, 'People can only love outside and can only kiss outside, but Mister God can love you right inside, and Mister God can kiss you right inside, so it's different.'[10] That is what the Eucharist is, God kissing us 'right inside'. You cannot explain a kiss or an embrace, but their power and beauty are undeniable; God's language of love eludes our heads, but not our hearts.

In the other sacraments, we receive sanctifying grace but the Eucharist is unique because it is the only sacrament in which we actually receive the person of Christ, in fact the whole Trinity.[11] Christ, the source of our holiness, is present before we receive the sacrament, 'Here, as with no other sacrament, the objective rite and the deepest subjective, emotional and mystical piety are united.'[12] Christ is the sacrament of God, and the Eucharist is the sacrament of Christ, which Elizabeth perceived in faith as a 'mysterious exchange' of love; everything was eclipsed as she immersed herself in her totally self-giving God. Her life and words have the ability to make the ineffable intimate, and she arouses our longings for this mystery of love.

God loves us and he wants to be loved in return. In the poem about her First Holy Communion, Elizabeth wrote of her desire to give her life completely to Christ, 'To return a little of His great love / To the Beloved of the Eucharist / Who rests in my poor heart.'[13] She reveals no more. In his spiritual autobiography, *Elected Silence*, Thomas Merton vividly describes his First Communion. Although separated by age, gender, nationality and culture, Merton captures something of what Elizabeth intimates in her poem:

> And my First Communion began to come towards me, down the steps. I was the only one at the altar rail. Heaven was entirely mine – that Heaven in which sharing makes no division or diminution. But this solitariness was like a reminder of the singleness with which this Christ, hidden in the small Host was giving Himself for me, and to me and with Himself, the entire Godhead and Trinity – a new increase of the power and grasp of their indwelling that had begun only a few minutes before at the font. In the Temple of God that I had just become, the One Eternal and Pure Sacrifice was offered up to the God dwelling in me: the sacrifice of God to God, and me sacrificed with God.[14]

St Peter Julian Eymard, Apostle of the Eucharist, says that this feeling of happiness in Jesus' presence is the first call; this initial grace grows imperceptibly and develops into a need and disposition whereby everything is directed towards the Eucharist. This perfectly describes Elizabeth's experience. Once she opened herself up to the Eucharist, it became the centre of her life, so that even in the midst of social gatherings she was absorbed by the thought of the following day's Holy Communion, for he fulfilled all the needs of her heart.

When Cardinal Hume visited Ethiopia, at the height of a famine, he felt overwhelmed both by the enormity of the misery and his seeming inability to do anything. He was touched to the core when a little boy took his hand and clung to it, gazing into his eyes, silently expressing his raw need for food and love. The

Cardinal reflected that, like the needy child, we all long for food, but even more for love, connection, intimacy.[15] In the Eucharist, Christ comes to us, answering the deepest hungers of the human heart and offering us a love we can believe in because he died for us; Love himself gave his life for us and continues to be with us, 'He is still living! Living in the tabernacle in His adorable Sacrament, living in our souls.'[16]

Continuing Communion

The desire to live in the eternal present, and live in ongoing, intimate communion with Love began for Elizabeth with Holy Communion. She understood that the life of a Carmelite aims to be one of uninterrupted communion with God, and this is true for every Christian:

> The life of a Carmelite is a communion with God from morning to evening, and from evening to morning. If He did not fill our cells and our cloisters, ah how empty they would be! But through everything we see Him for we bear Him within us, and our life is an anticipated Heaven. I ask God to teach you all these secrets.[17]

Elizabeth realized that, through the Eucharist, Christ establishes a communion of life with us so that we become another tabernacle wherein he rests and resides permanently. She shared this profound insight with everyone: Madame Angles, a lonely woman who suffered intensely; Germaine who wanted to be a Carmelite; married friends and anxious mothers. Elizabeth expressed her understanding with great clarity in a letter to Berthe who was preparing for her First Holy Communion, telling her that Jesus was not just coming to her for a few moments, but 'in order to remain with her always' and to 'remember that well' as their union had only just begun.[18] Elizabeth's words invite us to join with her in 'making our days a continual communion', for he is also within us as in a little host. Elizabeth loved praising God in the prayer of the Church, the Liturgy of the Hours, because it extends Eucharistic praise and thanksgiving throughout the day; everything flows from and leads to the Eucharist.

Adoration of the Blessed Sacrament

Elizabeth so appreciated the precious gift of Jesus in the Eucharist that even before entering Carmel she fervently spent time in the presence of the Blessed Sacrament. In a poem entitled *Perpetual Adoration,* written when she was eighteen, Elizabeth addresses Jesus of the Eucharist her Spouse, her Love and her Life:

> Jesus, God of the Eucharist
> Jesus, my support and my life
> Jesus, who deigns to choose me
> To love and console and to suffer. [19]

She loved to be in his Eucharistic presence, listening, speaking, consoling him.

In Carmel it meant much to Elizabeth to live under the same roof as the Blessed Sacrament and it is historically attested that she spent many hours in adoration, especially on Sundays and feast days. Eucharistic adoration was not originally a feature of the Teresian Carmel which, born of desert spirituality, under the inspiration of the great prophet Elijah, lays stress on the indwelling presence of God in pure faith. The frequency of Eucharistic adoration in the Dijon Carmel probably originated from Cardinal Bérulle and the French School of spirituality.

Elizabeth entered Carmel immediately after receiving Holy Communion, writing that only thus fortified by the Lord's presence could she bring herself to leave behind the mother whom she loved so much, and her beloved sister, the diffident Guite. She found them all again, and more deeply, in the presence of her Eucharistic Lord:

> Every Sunday we have the Blessed Sacrament exposed in the oratory. When I open the door and contemplate the divine Prisoner who has made me a prisoner in this dear Carmel, it seems to me rather like the gate of Heaven opening! Then I present to Jesus all those who are in my heart, and there, close to Him, I find them again . . . I do not regret these years of waiting: my happiness is so great it had to be paid for. Ah! How good God is! . . . Ask for me that holiness for which I thirst. [20]

Adoration of the Blessed Sacrament includes everyone; all are held, loved and embraced in his presence. We are reminded of Abba Dositheus who envisaged our journey towards Christ as a movement inward along the spokes of a wheel; we all begin on the rim, and as we move in towards Christ, who is the hub, we move closer to him and to each other. As Elizabeth reflects, 'He whom I possess within me also dwells in you so we are closely united.'[21] She writes to all those she loves of her widening horizons, proclaiming this wonderful presence of God. She arranges to rendezvous with her loved ones 'in Him';[22] 'in the Trinity';[23] 'in the Blessed Sacrament';[24] 'in the tabernacle';[25] 'in the infinity of God';[26] 'in His embrace';[27] 'Jesus is our rendezvous, our meeting place'.[28]

'Secret of the resurrection'[29]

The Eucharist is the transcendent meeting place where earth is united with heaven, the 'still point of the turning world'.[30] Elizabeth had a strong sense of the eschatological dimension of the Eucharist as the heavenly banquet during which we partake of the bread of heaven, the food of angels. Using a favourite expression, Elizabeth, describes the Eucharist as 'heaven in faith' reflecting, 'When I am near You / I do not believe that I am still on earth.'[31] The Church teaches that in the Eucharist we digest as it were, the 'secret of the resurrection'; in Holy Communion we enter into the eternal now. In the Eucharist we experience the eschatological tension whereby time past is contained in time present and time future is 'already' present though 'not yet' in its fullness; all this through our daily mystical encounter with our Risen Lord and God.

Christ's Transforming Presence

The beautiful insight that each one is a dwelling place, a tabernacle of God, has far-reaching implications. It encourages us to reverence not only ourselves, as Jesus does, for he comes to us daily, unconditionally, but also to respect others, for they, too, are tabernacles. Caryll Houselander once said that if we truly

believed in the presence of Christ in each other, we would genu-
flect before each person. Christ is present in us, regardless of age,
health, emotional stability, family background; he loves us and
comes to us, as we are, desiring to transform us, however, into
what we can become.

Elizabeth is a vibrant witness to the purifying and transforming
power of the Eucharist, whose effects are incalculable, 'We must
allow ourselves to be transformed / Into His image.'[32] The grace
of this wonderful sacrament gives spiritual nourishment; it stim-
ulates growth in the Christian life; it increases sanctifying grace
and weakens the inclination to sin. It cancels venial sins and
increases charity, binding us more closely in the Mystical Body,
the Church.[33] In Elizabeth, we see someone in whom all this was
accomplished and what is particularly encouraging is that she does
not seem to have experienced any extraordinary mystical graces.
Instead, she brought extraordinary love and devotion to the
Eucharist, which, according to Teresa of Avila and John of the
Cross, is what really matters; it is the stuff of real holiness.

For Elizabeth the Eucharist and transformation go hand in hand,
for Christ 'wants to consume our life in order to change it into his
own.'[34] It is the 'Law of Love'; a natural consequence of loving is
that we become like those we love. We do not just receive him to
contemplate him or to take him as a model. No, we turn to Christ
with confidence in his capacity to radically change our life into the
very life of God. Neither our attitude, nor our state of soul bring
this about, it is rather the transforming love of the living God,
which works miracles in our hearts. What counts for Elizabeth is
that, regardless of weakness and failure, we constantly return to
Christ. Like the Church Fathers, Elizabeth knew the Eucharist to
be a powerful medicine which heals and purifies, the means by
which we allow Christ to transform us so that we can truly become
a sacrament of Christ, 'He is within us to make us holy, so let us ask
Him to be Himself our holiness.'[35]

Sacramental Spirituality

When we participate fully in the Eucharist, we gradually develop
Eucharistic minds and hearts, so that our whole lives become the

sacrament we celebrate. This perception lies at the heart of Elizabeth's sacramental spirituality. For her the Carmelite is a sacrament of Christ. Her unwavering faith saw the presence of God in all the daily details of her existence; there could be no artificial separation between faith and life. Evelyn Underhill, another woman of faith for our times, echoes this:

> Bring your whole situation en bloc into your Godward life. Knock down the partition between living-room and oratory, even if it does mean tobacco smoke and incense get a bit mixed up.[36]

It is the only authentic way to live as a Christian. As Elizabeth expresses it:

> Each incident, each event, each suffering, as well as each joy, is a sacrament which gives the soul God; so it no longer makes a distinction between these things; it surmounts them, goes beyond them to rest in its Master, above all things.[37]

The true work of love is to see everything in God, as an outward sign of inward grace. Thus, everything becomes a sacrament, 'Let us make all our days a communion with the Lord.'[38] Elizabeth reminds us that the character of being baptized is to be reality and sacrament, sign and channel of grace. Once you are baptized you are a sacrament. Your life is, potentially, a sign and channel of grace for you and others. This is a profoundly significant aspect of our dignity as Christians which Elizabeth lived intensely and nowhere more so than in suffering.

'Suffering is your best prayer'[39]

The Eucharist brings a whole new perspective on suffering, which then becomes a privileged means of participating in Christ's sacrifice. Our society has robbed suffering of its dignity and potential, devaluing its meaning. Where there is suffering or imperfection, every effort is made to eradicate it, change it, make it perfect. Alleviating suffering is a Christian duty, but there is another aspect of the Christian vision which, through faith, sees the immense potential in suffering to be redemptive, in imitation of

Christ. We do not seek out suffering, but when it comes, it is not merely a human problem to be overcome at all costs, but offers us an opportunity for growth in holiness and intimacy with Christ. John of the Cross goes so far as to suggest that we cannot reach full transformation and union without suffering.

To a friend longing for union with God, Elizabeth encourages faith and acceptance of suffering as a privileged participation in the self-offering of Christ, celebrated in the Eucharist:

> At those times when you feel those terrible voids, believe that He is hollowing out in your soul greater capacities to receive Him, capacities which are, to an extent, as infinite as Himself. Try then, in your will, to be wholly joyful under the hand that crucifies you; I would even go so far as to say that you should look upon each suffering as a proof of love that comes to you directly from God in order to unite you to Him.[40]

Our trust in God's actions is our greatest act of worship. To trust him is to praise him.[41]

The saints take this to another plane entirely, expressly desiring suffering in order to prove their immense love for God and their yearning to be completely identified with Christ. This is Elizabeth's attitude to suffering which she imparts to others: welcome suffering because Jesus shares his cross with those he loves. She often quotes Teresa of Avila's prayer-motto, 'To suffer or die!'[42] With great insight, she suggests that there is something 'so great, so divine in suffering' that the blessed in heaven probably envy our capacity for suffering, because it is such a 'powerful lever on the heart of God.'[43] When we stay close to the crucified, suffering becomes our best prayer.

Suffering is always suffering, we cannot take it out of life; it happens to us all. We pursue a certain course and something quite unexpected, unavoidable and beyond our control, cuts across, 'a cross', our plans, forcing a change of direction and causing real pain. We struggle to deal with what life hurls at us, but our outlook is what ultimately makes the difference between frustration and peace, which is why Elizabeth recommends that we welcome suffering as a treasure and a most powerful prayer. We glimpse here Elizabeth's approach to her own suffering and how she transformed the appalling pain of her illness into something 'sweet to give Him'. While most of us would struggle to comprehend Elizabeth's courage, we humbly recognize the truth of her mystical perspective.

The Cross as Communion

In the year she entered Carmel, 1901, Elizabeth developed synovitis of the knee as a result of spending long hours kneeling in prayer. She had to keep her feet up for ten days which meant that she could not go to Mass. Elizabeth embraced this sacrifice as an opportunity to participate in Christ's suffering on the road to Calvary. However, the reason for her peaceful acceptance is both unexpected and revealing:

> I am deprived of Church and Holy Communion, but the good God does not need the Sacrament in order to come to me; I feel I have Him with me just as much. It is there in the depths, in the heaven of my soul that I love to find Him as He never leaves me: God in me, me in Him, oh that is my life.[44]

The maturity of this insight in one so young is astonishing: God's presence in her is so real that it is on a level with receiving him in the Eucharist. After Elizabeth received Holy Communion for the last time, her infirmarian asked how she coped without it, and Elizabeth revealed she had entered into a new form of communion, 'I find Him now on the cross, it is from there he gives me life.'[45]

Elizabeth understood and lived the Eucharist as both sacrifice and sacrament.[46] It is the memorial of the sacrifice on Calvary in which we are called to participate fully. Elizabeth lived her dying as a Mass, using sacramental language to interpret her experience. She demonstrates what it means to think and live sacramentally, 'This Mass He is saying with me, for which his love is the priest, may last a long time yet.'[47] Her bed of pain was her 'altar'; she was the host-victim and Mother Germaine her 'consecrating priest'.[48] Elizabeth's whole life was related to the four key actions of the Eucharist – take, bless, break and give – which encapsulate her entire spirituality. She became the Sacrament she had so loved and cherished throughout her life, a living sacrifice of praise.[49] Her illness, thereby, was a living Eucharist and it provides a perspective on suffering and death, which transforms them into privileged moments of Eucharist. One of her sisters once said that Elizabeth was prayer personified. We could add that she was Eucharist personified.

Elizabeth of the Eucharist

The opening words of *Ecclesia de Eucharistia* echo Elizabeth's Eucharistic spirituality so closely that we could easily substitute Elizabeth's name for the Church's, as everything the Pope says of the Church, is true of Elizabeth and, because she is so thoroughly Christian, it applies to us also:

> The Church draws her life from the Eucharist. This truth does not simply express a daily experience of faith, but recapitulates the heart of the mystery of the Church ... [Her gaze] is constantly turned to her Lord, present in the Sacrament of the Altar, in which she discovers the full manifestation of his boundless love.[50]

The Eucharist was everything to Elizabeth and her writings have the power to rekindle our appreciation of this beautiful gift, 'the sum and summary of our faith'.[51] We see how the Eucharist animated and empowered her, extending her horizons to the infinite, to eternity. It is the deepest source of her, and our, eschatological hope. In her, 'the theology of the Eucharist takes on the splendour of a lived reality; it becomes "contagious" and in a manner, it "warms our hearts."'[52]

Notes

1. *CCC* 1392, see *EdE* 17.
2. *LG* 11.
3. *CCC* 1324.
4. *EdE* 1, see 6.
5. *MF* 1.
6. *EdE* 62.
7. See *MF* 15.
8. *L* 165.
9. *GOS* 74.

10. Fynn, *Mister God,* p. 41.
11. See *MF* 38.
12. Vorgrimler, *Sacramental Theology*, p. 132.
13. *P* 47, *OC*, p. 958.
14. Merton, *Elected Silence,* p.180.
15. Hume, *The Mystery of the Cross,* p. 25.
16. *L* 184.
17. *L* 123.
18. *L* 112.
19. *P* 67, *OC*, p. 982.
20. *L* 91, see *EdE* 25.
21. *L* 170.
22. *L* 184.
23. *L* 252.
24. *L* 119.
25. *L* 116.
26. *L* 169.
27. *L* 289.
28. *L* 106.
29. *EdE* 18, see *MF5*.
30. Eliot, 'Burnt Norton', *Four Quartets,* l. 62.
31. *P* 67, *OC*, p. 983.
32. *PN* 14, *OC*, p. 905.
33. *CCC* 1391–8 passim, see *MF* 66–7.
34. *HF* 18.
35. *L* 184.
36. Williams, *The Letters of Evelyn Underhill.*
37. *HF* 10.
38. *L* 172.
39. *L* 207, see *GOS* 38.
40. *L* 249.
41. *Julian of Norwich*, ch. 10.
42. *Life,* ch. 40.
43. *L* 207.
44. *L* 62.
45. *Reminiscences,* p. 214.
46. See *MF* 34 and *EdE* 12.
47. *L* 309.
48. *L* 306.
49. See Rom. 12:1.
50. *EdE* 62
51. *CCC* 1327.
52. Ibid.

Elizabeth as a novice, 1902

Chapter 6

'Praise of Glory'

Whenever the soul hears herself being called by name, as
did Mary Magdalen at the tomb, the most personal and
unmistakable primal meaning of the personal God
resonates in the sound of one's name.

Hans Urs von Balthasar

Discovering Her New Name: 'Praise of Glory'

Elizabeth's understanding of her Christian and Carmelite vocation continued to evolve, particularly through her *lectio* of the
writings of 'the great St Paul'. She shared his overwhelming
passion for Christ, his Trinitarian spirituality and his absolute
fascination with the 'exceeding love' of God. She referred to St
Paul as the 'Father of her soul', and her enthusiasm for her
constant companion, guide and inspiration overflowed into her
letters which are filled with his teaching. Through him she discovered her 'new name', 'Praise of Glory', which marked another
great milestone in her spiritual life.

Elizabeth discovered her new name while reading the opening
liturgical hymn of Ephesians, one of the most profound medita-
tions in Scripture:

Blessed be the God and Father of our Lord Jesus Christ,
who has blessed us with all the spiritual blessings of heaven in Christ.
Before the world was made, he chose us, chose us in Christ,
to be holy and spotless, and to live through love in his presence,
determining that we should become his adopted sons and daughters
through Jesus Christ
for his own kind purposes,
to make us praise the glory of his grace,

His free gift to us in the Beloved,
in whom, through his blood, we gain our freedom,
the forgiveness of our sins.
Such is the richness of the grace
which he has showered on us
in all wisdom and insight.[1]

Elizabeth's Trinitarian heart responded to Paul's canticle exalting the gracious plan of redemption of the Father, Son and Spirit, who lovingly conspire to lavish blessings upon us. Caught up in this rapturous acclamation of God's wonderful plan of love, Elizabeth felt called to respond with equal love, not simply to praise him, but to become, in her very self a 'praise of His glory'. She had found her new name, 'Elizabeth of the Trinity, Praise of God's Glory', that personal name of Revelation by which we recognize God's most intimate call.[2]

'Words of destiny'[3]

No one before Elizabeth had considered this name and no one since has associated it with anyone but her; the two are inextricably linked. Through these 'words of destiny', God bestowed upon Elizabeth a unique vocation in the Church, to reveal a wonderful insight into our Christian calling. It further developed her name, Elizabeth of the Trinity, which no longer completely expressed her vocation, and with intimate friends, she subsequently signed herself *Laudem Gloriae*. This name, though grammatically incorrect, nevertheless signalled the ultimate development of Elizabeth's baptismal grace, to 'praise, reverence and serve God'.[4]

Elizabeth's contemplative heart was overwhelmed by the wonder of being chosen from all eternity to praise God's glory:

For those whom he foreknew he also predestined to be conformed to the image of his Son ... those whom he predestined he also called; and those whom he called he also justified; and those whom he justified he also glorified.[5]

She was equally enthralled by God's gracious love, encapsulated in Paul's 'gospel', 'through grace you have been saved',[6] and nearly all of her subsequent letters mention these key Pauline texts.

Elizabeth's new name was destined to become the focal point of her spirituality as she uncovered its meaning in the last suffering years of her life. One privileged aspect of her vocation as 'Praise of Glory' was to make him 'forget everything by the strength of [her] love.'[7] For Elizabeth, two words summed up all holiness and apostolate, 'Union and Love'.[8] To be a 'Praise of Glory' is to be totally, lovingly united with God. As Elizabeth's illness progressed, so did her understanding, and in 1905, she added the significant word 'sacrifice', aligning her self-offering with Christ's:

> When you consecrate the host in which Jesus, who alone is the Holy One, is about to become incarnate, would you consecrate me with Him, 'as a sacrifice of praise to His glory,' so that all my aspirations, all my movements, all my actions may be a homage rendered to His holiness?[9]

In her correspondence with the young curate, Abbé Chevignard, Elizabeth reflected on the similarity between the vocations of priest and Carmelite, both of whom were called 'to show forth God and give Him to souls.' He accomplished this through his priestly ministry, and she through her prayer. For both, 'sacrifice is only love put into action', and vocations further merge as all are called to be 'sacrificial beings'.[10] Thus, 'Praise of Glory' reveals even more strongly, the sacrificial and priestly dimensions of her vocation.

Heaven in Faith and The Last Retreat of the 'Praise of Glory'

Elizabeth's new name contained such richness that she furnished two 'portraits' of what it means to be a 'Praise of Glory'. The first, *Heaven in Faith*, a very lyrical, beautiful description, occurs at the end of the souvenir retreat notes written at the beginning of August 1906, for Guite, to help her to live her baptismal vocation as a wife and mother. The second, *The Last Retreat of the 'Praise of Glory'*, is an unflinching account of this demanding vocation. The third, probably most compelling image, is Elizabeth herself. These three portraits of a 'Praise of Glory' are the

culmination of years of prayer and self-giving, they speak powerfully from life to life. Like all last words, knowingly suffused with
the light of eternity, the two retreats provide an 'especially fascinating' spiritual testament for 'what we say in the face of immi-
nent silence' has unique power.[11] Von Balthasar comments that
all her earlier writings were but, 'preparation and beginnings.
Here her word is pure and flawless before God.'[12]

'The Creator's dream'[13]

God has a dream for us. Created in his image, his great dream for
each one of us is that we correspond to our vocation to become
the most beautiful likeness that is possible, 'perfect "Praises of
Glory" of the Most Holy Trinity.'[14] In an extended meditation,
which forms the spiritual climax of *Heaven in Faith*,[15] Elizabeth
meditates on the characteristics of a 'Praise of Glory of the Most
Holy Trinity' the 'great dream of the heart of God'.[16] Her
inspirational account describes the soul at the pinnacle of the spiritual life.

'A praise of glory is a soul that lives in God, that loves him with a pure, disinterested love'

A 'Praise of Glory' aims, primarily, to love with the highest kind
of love, the love that desires only the good of the Beloved. Elizabeth equates this with doing God's will, surrendering ourselves
'completely, passionately, so as to will nothing else but what God
wills.' In the *Last Retreat* she makes this explicit: a 'Praise of
Glory' is one who fulfils God's will.[17] What a difference there is
between doing God's will and doing it *as if it were* your own will;
the latter is the deepest union of wills possible, demanding total
commitment to the Other, with no thought for self. It is an
absolutely rugged spirituality animating 'acts of inflamed love'
which John of the Cross considers so precious that 'one of them
is more meritorious and valuable than all the deeds a person may
have performed in the whole of life without this transformation
[in love], however great they may have been.'[18]

'A praise of glory is a soul of silence that remains like a lyre under the mysterious touch of the Holy Spirit'

Elizabeth's musician's heart likens a 'Praise of Glory' to a lyre, the small, harp-like stringed instrument used in classical antiquity. This potent image conveys the sensitivity of a soul which silently awaits the creative touch of the master Musician, the Holy Spirit. The soul of silence is a perfect listener, for silence is the most intimate language of God. If earthly music transports the soul, think what heavenly music might do. A soul of silent prayer and adoration, especially the interior silence of mind, heart and will which roots the soul in God, is transformed into praise! Suffering is a special string on the lyre-soul that 'produces still more beautiful sounds' which move the heart of God. This is no ordinary instrument, but one utterly surrendered. In the depths of silent receptivity, the soul receives the 'inestimable blessings' which are most delicately bestowed by the Holy Spirit.

'A praise of glory is a soul that gazes on God in faith and simplicity'

While writing *Heaven in Faith,* Elizabeth was engrossed in reading a book, a gift from her mother, by the foremost Flemish mystic Jan van Ruysbroeck. She eagerly shares with Guite the spiritual vistas he is opening up to her. Ruysbroeck is enamoured of the wondrous simplicity of God and suggests a like simplicity as the beginning and end of all the virtues: a simplicity which places us in the presence of God; is the source of the spiritual life; gives light, hope and courage; silences inner noise and brings peace. It takes us into the inner abyss where we experience the touch of the Holy Trinity. This simplicity brings wholeness, harmony and, perfectly absorbed in God, radiates his beauty:

> And we, with our unveiled faces, reflecting like mirrors the brightness of the Lord, all grow brighter and brighter as we are turned into the image that we reflect; this is the work of the Lord who is Spirit.[19]

This mirroring of God will always reflect Christ. For Elizabeth, the concluding phase of her spirituality clearly grows out of the Trinitarian phase, just as, at the end of Dante's *Paradiso*, the face of the God-Man shines forth from the vision of the three inter-laced circles.

'A praise of glory is one who is always giving thanks'

Rolheiser, a modern spiritual master, equates thankfulness with holiness, 'To be a saint is to be motivated by gratitude, nothing more, nothing less', making 'ingratitude the original sin'.[20] Thankfulness is the primary virtue because it acknowledges that everything is grace. There is nothing that we are and have that is not totally and utterly gift. Yet we quickly forget and fall into pride and complacency, too easily taking things for granted. In contrast, the humble person has a childlike heart and lives in constant appreciation and wonder at the lavishness of God's generosity.

A 'Praise of Glory' has a Eucharistic heart, delighting in God's bounty in every moment, uniting herself in praise with the supreme act of thanksgiving, the Eucharist. Every Preface recalls the importance of thanking and praising God while weekday Preface IV conveys the sheer gift of our relationship with God:

> Father, all-powerful and ever-living God,
> we do well always and everywhere to give you thanks.
> You have no need of our praise,
> yet our desire to thank you is itself your gift.
> Our prayer of thanksgiving adds nothing to your greatness,
> But makes us grow in your grace,
> Through Jesus Christ our Lord.[21]

Where 'everything is grace', the only possible response is wonder, thankfulness and praise, which is why the Church prays Our Lady's *Magnificat* every evening.

The Last Retreat of the 'Praise of Glory'

The Last Retreat is much stronger in tone and content than the gentler *Heaven in Faith*. Mother Germaine asked Elizabeth to write down her spiritual insights during her final retreat, which Elizabeth designated, *The Last Retreat of the 'Praise of Glory'*, taking the opportunity to explain how she understood her work as a 'praise of glory'. It exhibits all the strength of an intellect and will which are totally dominated by faith, hope and love.

We cannot hope to grasp the mystical riches of *The Last Retreat* unless we recall the context. Elizabeth knows she is dying and she writes with the light of eternity beckoning. Her excruciating physical condition explains why the *Last Retreat* speaks so much of suffering. Elizabeth, in severe pain and unable to sleep, wrote in the lonely night hours familiar to every invalid. This is no abstract dissertation about suffering, but an intimate expression of love written from within almost unbearable pain. We are on holy ground when we read these words which reveal the depths of her inner life; they are the last testimony of a 'martyr of love'. Mother Germaine witnessed the indescribable transformation God was working in Elizabeth, during those days, which transcended even the mystical beauty and awesome asceticism of her words.

From the stark opening, '*Nescivi*', 'I knew not', [22] to the final paragraph, 'How beautiful is this creature thus stripped, freed from self',[23] Elizabeth outlines a rigorous ascetical programme of silence, faith, interior recollection and total death to self. In this spiritual masterpiece, Elizabeth is unrelenting in her war against self, revealing the austere secret of her spiritual progress, 'the condition [is]: we must be dead!'[24] *The Last Retreat* plunges us into the heart of John of the Cross' mystical theology, '*Nada, nada, nada,*' the unknowing which is the most potent form of knowing; that death to self and life in God, which is the purest 'song of the Praise of Glory!'[25]

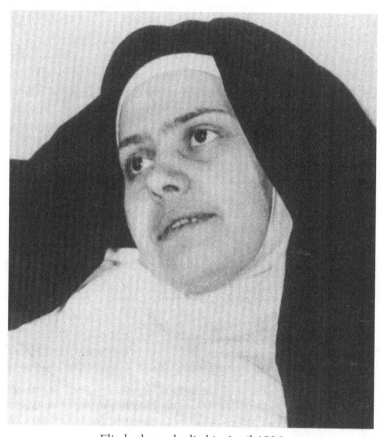

Elizabeth nearly died in April 1906

Redemptive Suffering

In the early part of *The Last Retreat*, Elizabeth reprises key elements of her spirituality, deepened and matured through suffering. Aquinas said that every choice is a renunciation. The only way to that 'complete self possession' which Elizabeth knew to be indispensable to the interior life, was a series of choices which unified the soul, directing it wholly to God. The soul that keeps anything for itself cannot be a perfect praise of glory, and that is what she desired. Simplicity, a singleness of purpose, creates a deep form of silence that withstands any disturbances, from without or within.

Unwavering faith provides the 'beautiful light', which is indispensable for inner unity: faith in God's love which is the deepest source of our joy. We give immense pleasure to God when we cling to him in the heaven of our soul with a simplicity of focus, through both joy and suffering, which restores us almost to a state of original innocence. Elizabeth shows us a way to reclaim ourselves, if we are willing to take it.

Elizabeth sees her suffering as an invitation to walk the way of the cross, by the side of her 'crucified, annihilated, humiliated King'. Suffering affects everyone. For believers, one of the most challenging and inspiring truths is that Christ, through his own suffering on the cross gave all suffering salvific meaning. Even more, Christ 'is present in every human suffering', gradually disclosing 'new horizons of the kingdom of God'.[26] Christians are not excused distress, even torment, but through Christ, sorrow is transformed into blessing so that, as Elizabeth discovers, she 'no longer suffers from suffering'.[27] The night of human weakness and pain is robbed of its terror, for not only does it not block our way, through the mysterious alchemy of faith, suffering is transformed into a message of God's glory.

'Adoration is a word from heaven'[28]

Adoration is the most perfect form of prayer because it is utterly Other-centred. The soul that dwells in the depths of God in unchanging peace, offers the interior adoration of the intellect and will, which is the most perfect form of praise. There is a passage from Teilhard de Chardin which could have been written by Elizabeth:

> ... what I cry out for, like every being, with my whole life and all my earthly passion, is something very different from an equal to cherish: it is a God to adore.
>
> To adore ... That means to lose oneself in the unfathomable, to plunge into the inexhaustible ... to annihilate oneself ... to give of one's deepest to that whose depth has no end ...
>
> The more man becomes man, the more will he become prey to a need, a need that is always more explicit, more subtle and more magnificent, the need to adore.[29]

Elizabeth is enraptured by the thought of transcending self in complete adoration of the holiness of God in imitation of Jesus, 'the perfect Praise of His Father's glory.'[30] 'Very few souls have had such a sense of this adoration in spirit and truth in the inner temple of the heart, as had Elizabeth ... a perfect adorer of God.'[31]

Overwhelmed by her desire to praise and adore, Elizabeth responds fully to God's invitation to be holy as he is holy. Fired with longing to live the perfection of God, Elizabeth strives to be unswerving in her efforts, reminding us of Cardinal Newman's observation that consistency is the hallmark of holiness. Elizabeth writes:

> I must keep myself always in the same state, the same isolation, the same retirement, the same detachment. If my desires, my fears, my joys, or my sorrows, if all the impulses coming from these four passions are not completely subjected to God, I shall not be solitary: there will be turmoil within me. Therefore, calm, the slumber of the powers, the unity of the whole being are needed.[32]

Time, place, and person are united in the peace of an eternal now. Always realistic, Elizabeth knows that only the 'sleep' of the 'noise within,' the overcoming of our distracting passions, can bring the solitude which enables the soul to listen attentively to the voice of God. His word will complete the stripping of the soul which will then resemble the Trinity! We become holy with God's holiness; this is our baptismal calling. The heaven of our soul then provides a fitting dwelling for 'the Three'.

'Crucified by love'

The Last Retreat gives no specific details of Elizabeth's inner struggles, but her repeated insistence on overcoming self-preoccupation, death to self, giving up self, ignoring self and looking at the Master, implies that she was engaged in an ongoing interior battle with self, as holiness does not bypass our humanity, grace always builds on nature. Her passionate temperament contributed to the richness of her life with God, but it must have often reared its more disturbing side. We recall Canon Angles' revealing insight, 'Elizabeth had all the more merit in that she was naturally lively, ardent and passionate.'

Elizabeth longed to be conformed to Christ, to share in his *kenosis*, self-emptying, in order to be transformed into a worthy bride for Him so that by the end of her life she reached absolute detachment. The Fourteenth Day is the darkest, most moving part of *The Last Retreat*, a stark and poignant commentary, in the words of her Saviour, written significantly in the third person, describing her own very real, personal crucifixion:

> In the hour of humiliation, of annihilation, she will remember these few words: 'Jesus suffered in silence'[33] and she, too, will be silent, 'keeping all her strength for the Lord',[34] the strength which we draw from silence.

> When the hour of abandonment, desertion and anguish comes, the hour that drew forth from Christ the loud cry: 'Why have you forsaken me?'[35] she will remember the prayer: 'That they may have my joy made complete in them';[36] and, drinking to the very dregs the chalice prepared by the Father,[37] she will find a divine sweetness in its bitterness.[38]

This graphic depiction of Elizabeth's suffering and spiritual identification with Jesus is expressed in the harsh language of his passion, for they both experienced the cross, and yet, paradoxically, both tasted 'divine sweetness'. He has destroyed every-thing only to 'clothe it with himself'. Elizabeth's acceptance of both joy and suffering as coming directly from Him, placed her soul on such serene heights that she intuited the joy of Jesus on the cross.[39]

Jesus has substituted Elizabeth for himself on the cross, and given her his Mother, 'to teach me to suffer as He did, to let me hear the last song of His soul which no one but His Mother could overhear.'[40] The *Last Retreat* moves from death to glory, as Eliza-beth reflects on the Blessed Virgin, 'the great Praise of Glory of the Holy Trinity', who will lead her home.

In Eric Gill's engraving of *The Trinity and the Chalice,* the Father's face is hidden behind Jesus dying on the cross, suggesting that to see the crucified Christ is to see the face of the Father, for Jesus is the great sacrament of God. The climax of Elizabeth's life lies in the simple recognition, 'He has ... substituted me for Himself on the Cross.'[41] She has fulfilled her 'dream of being transformed into Jesus crucified.'[42] In words she uses often, she is completely 'identified' with him, 'divinized',[43] and feels honoured to suffer with him, as she wrote to her mother:

> You fear that I am destined to be a victim of suffering; I beg of you not to grieve over what would be so beautiful. I feel unworthy of it! Just think what it would mean, to participate in the sufferings of my crucified Bridegroom; to go with Him to my passion; to share in His work of redemption![44]

It was said that, in her final days, Elizabeth looked like a living crucifix. Spiritually and physically, she had become 'Elizabeth the Crucified'. By implication, therefore, to look on the face of Elizabeth-Jesus, was to look on the face of the Father, for the just person

> Acts in God's eye what in God's eye he is –
> Christ – for Christ plays in ten thousand places ...
> To the Father through the features of men's faces.[45]

John of the Cross teaches that love shortens our stay on earth.[46] To invert Eliot's question, was what happened to Elizabeth a death or a birth? 'I had seen birth and death, / But had thought they were different'. [47] 'Elizabeth' is no more, 'I live now not with my own life but with the life of Christ who lives in me.'[48] She thus fulfilled her lifelong desire, to be Elizabeth 'disappearing, losing herself'.[49] She began in Christ, entered with him into the depths of the Trinity and ended in him; her *Prayer to the Trinity* was accomplished as Elizabeth was transformed into 'another humanity' in which his 'whole mystery' was renewed. Elizabeth's final name is 'Christ'. Our faith teaches that the life of a person reaches fulfilment when it most fully resembles Jesus: Elizabeth had reached holiness which is the foundation and summit of the spiritual life, thus completing the Father's eternal plan,

> A condition of complete simplicity
> (Costing not less than everything).[50]

Unceasing 'Praise of Glory'

How fitting that Elizabeth, 'House of God' should conclude her *Last Retreat* on the feast of the Dedication of the Churches of Carmel. The conclusion of the *Last Retreat of the 'Praise of Glory'* soars into the limitless wonder of heaven, to which we are all called. For Elizabeth, adoration was the 'ecstasy of love' and having shared that unique form of adoration, which is participation in the suffering of Christ, the 'perfect Adorer of the Father',[51] she anticipated dwelling in

> An eternal present . . . adoring Him always because of Himself, and becoming . . . the splendour of His glory, that is, the unceasing 'Praise of Glory' of His adorable perfections.[52]

This is the fullest development of Elizabeth's vocation as 'house of the God of Love', her, and our, eternal destiny. She discovered her deepest, truest self whose name is God, 'my *me* is God, nor do I know my selfhood save in Him'.[53]

Elizabeth invites us to become unceasing 'Praises of Glory' of the Blessed Trinity. Our response to her invitation could be expressed in the following prayer:

> May my life be . . .
> A 'Praise of Glory', as I live in God and love Him alone;
> A 'Praise of Glory', as a soul of silence;
> A 'Praise of Glory', as I gaze on God in faith and love and simplicity;
> A 'Praise of Glory', a Eucharistic soul, always giving thanks;
> A 'Praise of Glory', which lets go of self-preoccupation and loses itself in God;
> A 'Praise of Glory', of the Father, the Word and the Holy Spirit. Amen.

Notes

1. Eph. 1:3–8.
2. Rev. 2:17.
3. Balthasar, *Two Sisters,* p. 386.
4. Corbishley, *Spiritual Exercises of Saint Ignatius*, no. 23. See *CCC* 1701.
5. Rom. 8:29–30 (RSV). See *GV* 12; *HF* 23; *L* 231.
6. Eph. 2:5.
7. *L* 191.
8. *L* 191, see *L* 136.
9. *L* 244.
10. *L* 250, see *L* 256 and Underhill, *Mysticism*, p. 73.
11. Radcliffe, *Seven Last Words,* p. 3, see Bloom, *God and Man*, p. 68.
12. Balthasar, *Two Sisters*, p. 383.
13. *LR* 8.
14. *HF* 1.
15. Given in full at the end of the book. All quotations in this section are from there, p. 134, unless indicated otherwise.
16. *HF* 1.
17. *LR* 37–8.
18. *LF* 1.3.
19. 2 Cor. 3:18. See Ex. 33:7–11.
20. Rolheiser, *Infinite Horizon*, pp. 48ff.
21. *Weekday Missal,* p. 1052.
22. *LR* 1. See Balthasar, *Two Sisters*, p. 448.
23. *LR* 44.
24. *LR* 16.
25. *LR* 1.
26. *SD* 26.

27. *LR* 14.

28. *LR* 21.

29. Teilhard de Chardin, *Le Milieu Divin*, pp. 117–18.

30. *LR* 2.

31. *Reminiscences,* p. xxix.

32. *LR* 26.

33. See Mk. 15:5.

34. See Ps. 59:10.

35. Mk. 15:34.

36. Jn. 17:13.

37. Jn. 18:11.

38. *LR* 39.

39. See *GV* 4; *HF* 20; Nicholl, *Holiness*, p. 144.

40. *LR* 41.

41. Ibid.

42. *L* 324.

43. *L* 231, *L* 274.

44. *L* 300.

45. 'As Kingfishers catch fire', *Gerard Manley Hopkins Selected Poems and Prose*, p. 51.

46. *LF* 1.34, see *L* 293.

47. 'Journey of the Magi', Eliot, *Selected Poems,* p. 98.

48. Gal. 2:20.

49. *L* 172.

50. Eliot, 'Little Gidding', *Four Quartets*, ll. 253–4.

51. *LR* 2.

52. *LR* 44.

53. St Catherine of Genoa, '*Vita e Dottrina*', in Underhill, *Mysticism*, p. 151.

Elizabeth after her Solemn Profession, 1903

Chapter 7

The Gift of Prayer

The devout Christian of the future will either be a mystic
or will cease to be anything at all.
Karl Rahner

Distinguishing Mark of a Christian

At the beginning of the new millennium, John Paul II challenged
the Church to 'launch out into the deep' and follow Christ with
renewed energy and for this we need 'training in holiness',[1] especially in prayer, which should be the distinguishing mark of a
Christian. Prayer is not something we do, it is something God
does in us, and only when we humbly acknowledge that, on our
own, we are incapable of prayer are we ready to receive freely the
gift of prayer. The heart of our faith is the conviction that God
loves us. When we take this seriously, we respond to God's love
through a relationship formed and sustained in prayer. Prayer
then becomes something we are because, 'prayer and Christian
life are inseparable'.[2]

Simple, Deep, Encouraging and Possible

Although we know that prayer is God's gift, we sometimes feel
uncertain about how to engage in prayer. Elizabeth's teaching on
prayer is particularly helpful because it is simple, deep, encouraging and possible. Even in her youth, her friends were fascinated
by her absorption in and love of prayer, so much so that after
watching her pray, they were encouraged to pray more themselves. She is a powerful apostle of prayer, because everything she
writes is rooted in her own lived experience. If we patiently and

sincerely follow her advice, therefore, she will lead us to the innermost depths of ourselves where we will find our true home in God, who dwells within, longing for us.

Elizabeth gives no method or systematic teaching on prayer, instead she goes straight to the essence: to pray is to encounter God's living presence within, 'you have him so close to you. Desire him there, adore him there.'[3] Elizabeth shows us that deep prayer is possible for everyone because the theological virtues of faith, hope and love, infused by our baptism, give us the capacity to know and love God. We are born contemplative, therefore prayer is not just possible, it is essential. In the film *Shadowlands*, C. S. Lewis' prayer for his dying wife's recovery seems to have been heard, yet when asked if he is pleased, he gives a totally unexpected response:

> That's not why I pray . . . I pray because I can't help myself. I pray because I'm helpless. I pray because the need flows out of me all the time, waking and sleeping. Prayer doesn't change God, it changes me.[4]

We pray because God is God and we cannot live without prayer. The important thing is to want to pray; our desire for prayer is prayer, 'to desire *is* to possess God',[5] and when we give God time and space, he will take care of the rest, for it is impossible for God not to act if we do our part.[6] We learn to pray by praying.

Faith and Feeling in Prayer

Elizabeth cuts across our human tendency to complicate prayer, basing her teaching on the trusting prayer which is evoked by the most contemplative of psalms, and a favourite of St Thérèse:

> O Lord, my heart is not proud, nor haughty my eyes.
> I have not gone after things too great
> Nor marvels beyond me.
> Truly I have set my soul in silence and peace.
> As a child has rest in its mother's arms,
> even so my soul.[7]

A child does not have to do anything to be loved, and I am always a beloved child of God. His love is unconditional: it does not depend on who I am, how I am or what I have done. When I feel dry, bored or simply weary, and prayer feels like a waste of time, I may be tempted to stop praying. Elizabeth also had her struggles in prayer, and relates how sometimes she found prayer so hard that she wanted to run out of choir. On another occasion she admitted, 'How hard and difficult ordinary prayer seems; it is painful to have to work hard to draw into unity one's powers, and how it costs and seems difficult!'[8] Her struggles in prayer taught her an invaluable lesson, that the seeming inability to pray, which she had found so hard, became a blessing because the experience taught her the truth of her dependence on God. As Augustine said, 'Man is a beggar before God.'[9] Wisely, Elizabeth continued praying, no matter the cost, following Teresa of Avila's advice never to abandon prayer, no matter what we feel, because persevering in prayer is the only way to remedy the situation. This leads us to a vital truth in the spiritual life: we cannot gauge prayer by our feelings. Faith, hope and love transcend feelings; it is the will that counts:

> It does not matter whether you are feeling fervent or discouraged: we pass from one state to another in this earthly exile. You must believe that He never changes; that in His care for you He is always bending over you, longing to bear you away and establish you within Himself.[10]

When life is tough and faith feels fragile, Elizabeth urges us to 'cling to God through everything' in trust, aware of the power of this simple gesture.[11] On her deathbed, Elizabeth promised to help souls to cling to God rather than the self, or the myriad other trifles which undermine resolve, diverting us from his loving presence. Her vivid language suggests the tenacity of Teresa of Avila's 'determined determination', whereby we simply hang on. In a society where we tend to 'move on' rather than 'hang on' and everything seems to be disposable, including people, we are in danger of losing sight of the value of constancy. Our commitment to prayer in times of dryness and difficulty is itself an immensely powerful prayer, for 'perseverance wounds the heart of God.'[12]

Love is a decision not a feeling and we can never measure prayer by how we feel, but by its transforming effects, as it is the silent source of growth. Furthermore, John of the Cross tells us that when God seems most absent he is, paradoxically, most present, communicating himself at a deeper level. If we, like the Prodigal Son, move towards him in faith and love, then he like the Prodigal Father, will come the rest of the way. A look, a movement of the heart, the mind, the body, a barely articulated desire, presence: all this is prayer.

'We must be so simple!'

Elizabeth is very insistent on this, telling her mother to be completely candid with God and simply pour out her heart to him, for it is not the form of our prayer or the words we use that matter. God does not need our fancy words or clever thoughts. In fact, 'thinking [often] gets you nowhere'.[13] He simply wants us to be with him. Elizabeth advises young Germaine always to love *prayer*, not reciting lots of vocal prayers, but that 'endless dialogue' which is a silent 'being with'. Elizabeth personifies Teresa's key insight, in prayer, 'The important thing is not to think much but to love much.'[14]

At times of illness and anxiety when we need God more, we often feel less able to pray and this is when the habit of prayer carries us through. Elizabeth corresponded with Madame Angles, an invalid who was full of good intentions but felt weighed down by her illness. Elizabeth is so reassuring, to be with God just as we are, is prayer: 'It is so simple! He is always with you. Be always with Him, in your actions, your sufferings, and when your body is exhausted. Remain in His sight; see Him present with you, living in you.'[15] When Mme Catez was unwell, housebound and feeling lonely, Elizabeth encouraged her to take advantage of the enforced inactivity to enjoy the solitude and find rest in the arms of God, to let him 'fill, invade everything . . . I think we must be so simple with the good God.'[16] When friends wrote to her, begging prayer for the sick and infirm, she promised to entrust the needy person lovingly to the Lord in prayer, saying quite simply to him, 'The one you love is ill.'[17]

It is tempting to want to present ourselves as devout, articulate and impressive, but Elizabeth will have none of it. Prayer only deepens when we 'let our masks fall' and approach God without posturing or pretence, humbly surrendering ourselves to the God who has first surrendered himself to us.[18] Our desire to please him does in fact please him. Prayer is that simple; we need to be humble enough to pray as we are and leave the rest to God.

When Guite is wearied by her human fragility and struggling with faith, Elizabeth uses the experience of her children's trust, to teach her a beautiful lesson about abandonment to God:

> If Jesus seems to sleep, let us rest beside Him; let us be calm and silent; do not let us wake Him, but wait in faith. I do not think that while Sabeth and Odette are in their mother's arms they trouble themselves much as to whether there is sunshine or rain; let us imitate the little ones and rest in the arms of God with the same simplicity.[19]

We mistakenly think we can only pray when we are fresh and eager. Elizabeth urges us to pray at all times. When she felt dejected, she followed her own advice, 'Go and be consoled by Him during the times when we feel only our miseries, and I am so full of them!'[20] When Elizabeth's health failed and she spent time alone in the garden, she wrote to Guite, 'I am going to bury myself in the depths of my soul, that is, in God. Will you imitate me in this very simple movement?'[21] Notice Elizabeth's tact in gently slipping in her invitation to Guite, to make 'this very simple movement' towards him, which is the essence of prayer. Through trusting God in prayer, we come home and find deep 'rest and relaxation'. Allowing ourselves to be drawn gently inward to rest in God, becomes the beginning and end of prayer. Elizabeth's insights echo those of the popular English mystic, Julian of Norwich, 'the best prayer is to rest in the goodness of God.'[22]

'Fix your gaze on God'

Elizabeth loved to pray from an early age and asked God to make her whole life a continual prayer, one long act of love. Immersed

Elizabeth's farewell photo, just before entering Carmel

in the teaching of Teresa of Avila, Elizabeth tells friends to gaze on God, contemplating him with a 'wholly loving look', and she particularly recommends gazing at the cross of Christ as a most powerful prayer, a practice also favoured by Cardinal Hume. Doing everything 'under the Divine gaze', remaining always in his presence, gazing on God with our lives, is prayer. Imperceptibly, prayer becomes as simple and necessary as breathing. When Elizabeth entered Carmel she was delighted to find God everywhere, 'We live Him and breathe Him,'[23] touching on an important reality, that we are held in being by God's 'kiss of life'.

In the *Spiritual Canticle,* John of the Cross explains that in the highest state of union, every inbreath of the soul is an outbreath of God.[24] This is also true of the early stages of intimacy. Continual prayer is being consciously in the presence of him, in whom 'we live, and move and exist.'[25] If applied to God, the words of the 60's love song, capture something of this deep theological truth:

> You're my world, you're every breath I take,
> You're my world, you're every move I make . . .
> If our loves ceases to be,
> Then it's the end of my world for me.

Prophet of the Presence of God

In *Letters to Malcolm,* C. S. Lewis says that any patch of sunlight will show you something about the sun that you could never get from books. Elizabeth's life is a 'patch of Godlight', which shines forth the precious truth of the presence of God. John Paul II acclaimed Elizabeth as a 'prophet of the presence of God' and one of her most precious gifts to the Church is the way she makes this presence so real. She reminds us that, through baptism, we each have the wonderful reality of the presence of God dwelling within; she rekindles our faith, awakening our desire to live in the presence of God ourselves and become the presence of God for others. Those who visited her in Carmel said that it was 'impossible to come near her without being impressed and penetrated with the presence of God . . . grace seemed to pass from her through the grille.'[26]

Elizabeth believed so passionately in the presence of God that everything she says about prayer centres on this fundamental reality, 'God in me and I in him that is my life.'[27] She promises to ask, 'the Holy Spirit to reveal . . . the presence of God within you.'[28] Elizabeth is flexible about how we live this presence of God, telling her mother that it does not matter whether she thinks of God as within her or close to her. What matters is not *how* we envisage this presence, but *that* we believe and dwell in it, for this is prayer.

Like Gregory of Nazianzus, she knows that we must make time for prayer as we cannot hope to pray at all times if we do not pray at specific times. She gives very practical advice for developing the habit of continual prayer, recalling Brother Lawrence, the humble Carmelite who spent forty years as a hard-working lay brother, practising the presence of God. Both Carmelites encourage us to live from the heart, not the head, keeping loving company with the Lord in all the mundane duties and happenings, making prayer possible at all times. Elizabeth gives family and friends solid guidance to sustain them on the path of prayer. In the postscript of a letter, she reminds her mother to take advantage of a forthcoming train journey as an opportunity for prayer, and in another letter, to consciously recollect herself from time to time and pray in five-minute snatches. In other words, to do everything possible to introduce the habit of prayer into everyday life, raising the mind and heart to God through everything, which establishes us in God's presence.

Prayer in the 'Cell of the Heart'

While waiting to enter Carmel, Elizabeth imitated St Catherine of Siena who, 'always dwelt in her cell even when in the midst of the world, for she lived in that inner dwelling-place.'[29] Elizabeth loved this idea and found it so helpful that she advised others to create a 'cell of the heart' as a way of living in the presence of God.

Lack of opportunity and space can often prevent us from spending time in prayer, but building a 'little cell' within allows us endless opportunities for those brief, or extended, moments of encounter which sustain our relationship with God. Elizabeth knew from experience that it is not always possible to find a church to pray in, whereas this inner cell provides a permanent place of encounter. John of the Cross teaches, moreover, that our innermost centre, the substance of the soul, is totally protected by God, placed by him beyond the reach of our feelings, senses or the devil.[30] Nothing can prevent us being present to the God who dwells in this most sacred space, which is ours by virtue of our baptism. It is our sanctuary and refuge, even, at times, from ourselves. When feeling stressed or unhappy, people talk of taking time out but the real secret of happiness is to take time within. Elizabeth writes to Françoise, a difficult young woman, but one whom she understood so well, because they had similar temperaments:

> Build a little cell within your soul as I do. Remember that the good God is there, and enter it from time to time. When you feel anxious or unhappy, seek refuge there at once and confide every-thing to the Divine Master.[31]

Elizabeth cleverly uses their friendship as a model for Françoise's relationship with God. She continues, 'You used to sit beside me and tell me all your secrets, that is how you ought to be with Him.'[32]

Heart-to-Heart

All true religion is of the heart. Teresa of Avila described prayer as 'an intimate sharing between friends'.[33] Elizabeth described prayer as a heart-to-heart, recalling Cardinal Newman's motto, *cor ad cor loquitur* (heart speaks to heart) and she would have welcomed this beautiful meditation on the heart in the *Catholic Catechism*:

> The heart is the dwelling-place where I am, where I live; accord-ing to the Semitic or biblical expression, the heart is the place 'to which I withdraw'. The heart is our hidden centre, beyond the grasp of our reason and of others; only the Spirit of God can fathom the human heart and know it fully. The heart is the place

of decision, deeper than our psychic drives. It is the place of truth where we choose life or death. It is the place of encounter, because as image of God we live in relation: it is a place of covenant.[34]

In prayer, Elizabeth lets her heart go, saying a million things to her divine Spouse, knowing that he also delights in this heart-to-heart. This is what life is about, what we are made for, relationship with the One who loves us. Once we have that, we have everything, which is why Elizabeth could write:

> Then what does it matter how He wishes me to employ myself, since He is always with me? Prayer, the heart-to-heart, must never end. I feel Him so alive in my soul! I have only to recollect myself to find Him within, and this is the source of all my happiness. He has placed in my heart a thirst for the infinite and such a great need for love that He alone can satisfy![35]

Creating a 'Cell of the Heart'

Enthusiastic responses to the Carthusian film *Into Great Silence* indicate the impressive, if daunting, beauty of recollection and silence in which the viewer is immersed. It touched a chord, for we sense that silence is the most appropriate language for apprehending God; all else is but a poor translation.[36] Elizabeth knew this intuitively and emphasized the absolute necessity of recollection. In the spiritual classics, *The Way of Perfection* and *The Interior Castle*, Teresa of Avila devotes several chapters to the importance of the prayer of recollection, 'This prayer is called "recollection" because the soul collects its faculties together and enters within itself to be with its God.'[37] John of the Cross goes so far as to say that the intensity of God's loving inflow is actually determined by the soul's preparation.[38] Recollection is the antithesis of distraction and without it there can be no growth in God and prayer.[39] We can only truly know ourselves and God when, through recollection, we live from within. Our culture seems uncomfortable with silence. The rush, noise and endless diversions, the cacophony of aural, physical and visual noise exhaust us and drown out the 'still, small voice'. During *The Last Retreat,* Elizabeth meditates on John of the Cross' strong image of 'the invisible fortress of holy recollection',[40] encouraging us to reclaim ourselves, entering within the silence which is our deepest self in God.

Knowledge on the Path of Prayer

In *The Interior Castle,* Teresa of Avila, the most human of saints, laments the damaging effects of lack of knowledge on the path of prayer. The real trouble is that we do not even recognize our ignorance and, therefore, do not know what advice to seek.[41] Francis Bacon's maxim, 'knowledge is power' is particularly true of the spiritual life where lack of knowledge often leads to great suffering and discouragement. Growth in self-understanding, conversely, makes us tolerant of our own failings and compassionate with others, enabling us to direct our energies more effectively.

Deepening Levels of Silence

John of the Cross presents three stages of acquiring deep interior solitude in the soul's centre. It may be helpful to imagine three concentric circles, each area representing a layer of noise-silence. Achieving the first level of exterior silence and recollection requires a going in, a withdrawal into our selves, a distancing from the outer noise of the senses, with their kaleidoscope of sights, sounds, smells, etc., by means of which our natural desires entice, attract and dissipate our energies. Today's world bombards us with so much noise that it is difficult to find quiet and great efforts are required to control our senses in order to achieve the first layer of silence, which is still only external. Selecting a peaceful room and becoming physically still, allowing the body to sink into stillness creates a climate of inner calm, which is conducive to prayer.

Things take time; growth cannot be hurried. The danger of our fast-paced society is not just its speed, but rather the illusion it creates that everything can be accomplished instantly, which is manifestly untrue. We sense the frightening truth of Pascal's statement, 'All human evil comes from a single cause, man's inability to sit still in a room on his own.' Unless we learn how to sit still, in silence, in peace, on our own, we will remain strangers to ourselves. Only in recollection do we 'recover ourselves and resume our true identity' in God.[42] It takes time to be still, enter into silence, and learn how to wait on God. Nature teaches us that the silence of the garden is the silence of growth.

The Battle Must be Fought

Achieving the next level of silence, however, is more challenging because it involves entering more deeply within, battling with our hectic thoughts, and uncontrolled passions, the 'stones and debris' which 'block the entrance'.[43] Teresa of Avila, tormented by distractions, acknowledges that we can no more stop the movement of our unpredictable minds than we can control the heavens. Our 'monkey mind', as Buddhists term it, jumps from thought to thought, ever restless and unruly, seemingly incapable of remaining in the present moment. The four passions, our sorrows, hopes, joys, and fears, overwhelm us by their intensity, relentlessly tossing us about. Elizabeth, immersed in John of the Cross, describes the ensuing inner chaos that we all recognize so well:

> A soul which argues with itself, which is preoccupied with its feelings, pursuing useless thoughts and desires, scatters its forces, for it is not totally ordered to God. Its lyre is not in tune and when the Divine Master touches it, He is not able to produce divine harmonies. It is still too human and discordant.[44]

This passage describes something of Elizabeth's struggle for recollection and authentic silence. Overcoming the self-centred inner clamour takes time, effort and patience and, above all, the grace of God. The inner turmoil of mind and feelings subsides and the soul gradually enters the second layer of silence. At this point, a certain self-possession is achieved in the presence of the Peaceful One for, 'We pray as we live and we live as we pray.'[45] Wisdom and honesty are required to discern when overpowering thoughts, emotions or events are an invitation to growth and need to become part of our prayer, held before the enlightening, calming and healing gaze of God, or when simply and peacefully to let them go.

Waiting on God

Nothing hurts like waiting, but there is no substitute for it in the spiritual life, as it takes us into the third level of silence. When Carlo Carretto, author of the spiritual classic, *Letters from the Desert,* was asked what he had learned from all his years of silence and prayer in the Saharan desert, he replied, 'to wait – wait – wait for God, wait for love, to be patient with everything. Everything that is worthwhile must be waited for!'[46] Infected as we are by a push-button culture which exalts instant communication, information and results, waiting feels like wasting valuable time. Conditioned by the mentality of this present world to believe that we should either be doing something or planning something, waiting can make us feel anxious and uneasy and we have to fight the negative pull of our culture and 'give ourselves permission' to wait on God.

Model for Interior Souls

For Elizabeth, Mary is *the* model of the humble one, waiting, treasuring everything in her heart. During the season of Advent, she was particularly inspired by Mary:

> The attitude of the Virgin during the months that elapsed between the Annunciation and the Nativity is the model for interior souls ... in what peace, in what recollection Mary lent herself to everything she did! How even the most trivial things were divinised by her! For through it all the Virgin remained the Adorer of the gift of God ... never did the ineffable vision that she contemplated within herself in any way diminish her outward charity.[47]

L'attente, waiting for God is the attitude of the humble. Simone Weil believed that the ability to wait patiently, as an expression of obedience to the truth, is the foundation of the spiritual life.[48]

Waiting is a form of remembering God's longing for us; he is always present, waiting patiently at the door of our hearts, knocking, as Holman Hunt depicts so movingly in his painting, *Light of the World*. Christ always stands at the door of our hearts, strong, persistent, waiting to be allowed in. Elizabeth cannot bear to leave him outside and writes, 'Open your heart wide and welcome Him as your guest.'[49]

Elizabeth encourages her mother to persevere in waiting on God's presence, and to live in her depths, knowing from experience that God cannot resist our efforts:

> I wish I could tell all souls what sources of strength, of peace, and of happiness they would find if they would only consent to live in this intimacy. Only they don't know how to wait: if God does not give Himself in some perceptible way, they leave His holy presence and when God comes to give gifts, He finds no one there, the soul is outside of itself in exterior things, it is not living in its depths![50]

Perseverance in prayer takes us to the most intimate layer of silence, into the memory, understanding and will, the innermost part of ourselves. Elizabeth explains this very clearly:

> He wants you to go out of yourself, to give up all that preoccupies you, in order to withdraw into the solitude He has chosen as His dwelling place in the depths of your heart. He is always there, even when you do not feel it. He is waiting for you and wants to establish a 'wonderful exchange' with you ... Through this continual contact with you, He can deliver you from your weaknesses, your faults, from all that troubles you. Nothing can prevent you going to Him.[51]

Within this inner world of profound silence, we experience God in a way that transcends words and feelings, the 'sounding solitude' of pure faith.[52] The will is established in God, and we attain the closest union possible in this life for we are totally given to God, and the soul experiences great happiness. Gradually, the deepest level of silence within our innermost depths becomes an enduring state, which persists independently of outer, or indeed, inner noise. This is the deepest level of silence, wherein love becomes pure presence and listening, as 'Words, after speech, reach / into the silence.'[53]

Passion to Listen

The most important prayer in Judaism, the *Shema Israel,* and arguably the most influential monastic rule in Christendom, *The Rule of St Benedict*, both begin with the word, 'Listen!' In a world submerged by the sound of words, the sound of silence is conspicuously absent, consequently there is little listening. Silence and waiting, not ends in themselves, are the environment in which we learn and practise listening to our inner self, to God. The body is stilled, the mind and passions silent, and the heart readied to listen. To 'hold firm in faith' the soul remains 'wholly vigilant under its Master's gaze, wholly recollected as it listens to His creative word.'[54] The more Elizabeth encounters God, the more she longs to listen to him, prompting her to write earnestly to Abbé Chevignard:

> Do you not have a passion to listen to Him? Sometimes it is so strong, this need to be silent, that I would like to do nothing else but remain at the Saviour's feet, like Magdalene, eager to hear everything and to penetrate more and more deeply the mystery of love that He came to reveal.[55]

And what does she most deeply hear in this prayer of silent love? In this attentive silence, the soul perceives the Father speaking the incarnate Word, expressed most profoundly and succinctly by St John of the Cross:

> The Father spoke one Word, which was His Son,
> And this Word He always speaks in eternal silence,
> And in silence it must be heard by the soul.[56]

God speaks his Son in love, and as Love. The purpose of prayer is to open up our hearts, so that we may truly 'fall in love with God'.[57] Pure contemplation lies in receiving, and when we hear this Word uttered in love in the depths of our hearts, we are graced, like Elizabeth, with the most profound self-revelation of God. Then her prayer becomes ours, 'Word of my God, I want to spend my life in listening to You.'

Prayer of Christ

True prayer transforms the praying heart, enlarging its horizons. Elizabeth was fascinated by the implications of our union with Christ, 'Just as I love God with his own love so, too, I pray to him with his own prayer', for 'I have in me the prayer of Jesus Christ, the Divine Adorer.'[58] Writing to assure Canon Angles of her prayer, she exclaims:

> I feel that all the treasures of the soul of Christ belong to me, so that I am infinitely rich; and how overjoyed I am to draw from this source for all those I love and who have done good to me.[59]

In her identification with Christ, Elizabeth was very conscious of her apostolate of prayer. She understood the call of every Christian to share in Christ's ministry as prophet, priest and king, especially through prayer, which is infinitely rich as we pray in the power of Christ 'who prays in us as our head.'[60] She reflects on the secret power that emanates from a contemplative heart immersed in God, whose horizons expand to intercede for the healing and reconciliation of the whole of humanity. She writes to a young priest from Dijon, who has been sent to China, as a missionary:

> I want to be an apostle with you, from the depths of my dear solitude in Carmel, I want to work for the glory of God, and for that I must be wholly filled with Him; then I will be all powerful: one look, one desire will be an irresistible prayer that can obtain everything, since it is, so to speak, God whom we are offering to God ... Apostle, Carmelite, it is all one! Let us be all His.[61]

Elizabeth alerts us to the potential of our prayer, wanting us to endow our prayer with the same vitality. John of the Cross' *Prayer of a Soul Taken with Love,* perfectly expresses the awesome breadth of Elizabeth's insights:

> Mine are the heavens, and mine is the earth; mine are the peoples, the just are mine, and mine the sinners; the angels are mine, and the Mother of God, and all things are mine, and God himself is mine and for me, because Christ is mine and all for me.[62]

'Prayer personified'

How did this young woman acquire such spiritual wisdom? Readers are astonished to learn from the Dijon Carmel that Elizabeth never studied theology or spirituality. Evagrius, a fourth-century monk famous for his wisdom, teaches that if you pray you will be a theologian. Prayer takes us to the heart of reality, God's and our own: he will teach us everything we need to know in order to grow in him:

> In prayer we discover what we already have. You start from where you are and you deepen what you already have, and you realise that you are already there. We already have everything but we don't know it and don't experience it. Everything has been given to us in Christ. All we need is to experience what we already possess.[63]

Her sisters said that Elizabeth was 'prayer personified'. She continues to be a living witness to the power of prayer. Like Jesus, she teaches us by example. How much we need her mission today, to move us away from self-centredness, towards our inner life with God. She shows us what can happen when we take God seriously in our lives, surrendering ourselves to him in prayer. Through prayer, we fall in love with God, we stay in love with God and we become God.

Notes

1. *NMI* 32.
2. *CCC* 2745.
3. *C* 1.8.
4. From the film.
5. *LF* 2.23.
6. *LF* 3.46.
7. Ps. 131.
8. *Reminiscences,* p. 44, see *CCC* 2732–4.
9. *CCC* 2559.
10. *L* 249.
11. *L* 122.
12 *L* 235.
13. Hillesum, *An Interrupted Life,* p. 56.

14. *IC* IV.1.7.
15. *L* 138.
16. *L* 169.
17. Jn. 11:3.
18. *CCC* 2710.
19. *L* 239.
20. *L* 225.
21. *L* 239.
22. *Julian of Norwich*, ch. 5.
23. *L* 89.
24. *C* 39.3.
25. Acts 17:28
26. *Reminiscences*, p. 107.
27. *L* 62.
28. *L* 273.
29. *L* 239.
30. *LF* 1.9.
31. *L* 123.
32. Ibid.
33. *Life*, 8.5.
34. *CCC* 2563.
35. *L* 169.
36. *LF* 2.21, see *CCC* 2717.
37. *Way* 28.4.
38. *LF* 2.2.
39. Hildebrand, *Transformation in Christ*, p. 105.
40. *Reminiscences*, p. 250.
41. *IC* IV.1.9, see *CCC* 2726.
42. Hildebrand, *Transformation in Christ*, p. 108.
43. Hillesum, *An Interrupted Life*, p. 53.
44. *LR* 3.
45. *CCC* 2725.
46. Rolheiser, *Infinite Horizon*, p. 45.
47. *HF* 40.
48. Weil, *Waiting for God*, p. 47, see *CCC* 2727.
49. *L* 210.
50. *L* 302.
51. *L* 249.
52. *C* st. 15.
53. Eliot, 'Burnt Norton', *Four Quartets*, ll. 139–40.
54. *LR* 34.
55. *L* 158.
56. 'Maxims and Counsels' 21. See *CCC* 2717.
57. *NMI* 33.
58. *P* 88, see *CCC* 2740–1.

59. *L* 91.
60. *CCC* 2616.
61. *L* 124.
62. *CWJC* p. 669. See Balthasar, *Two Sisters,* p. 425.
63. Merton, in Laird, *Into the Silent Land*, p. 53, see *2A* 1.1, *3A* 14.2.

Last photo taken of Elizabeth before she died, 1906

Chapter 8

Always Believe in God's Love

Always believe in His Love.
He loves you today as
He loved you yesterday and as
He will love you tomorrow.[1]
Elizabeth of the Trinity

'God is free from all save His love'

Once, after celebrating the mysteries of Holy Week and Easter, Elizabeth reflected deeply on a thought popular in the Dijon Carmel, 'God is free from all save His love.'[2] This amazing statement delighted her mystical soul. Theology teaches us that God is all-powerful, all-loving, all-everything and that our prayer and praise cannot add anything to him, otherwise he would not be God. However, by a wonderful generosity of spirit, God loves us to such an extent that he places himself at our disposal and thereby makes himself vulnerable. This is an incredible insight. Taken to its logical conclusion he can even be hurt by us, as he was on the cross. Theology and mysticism seem to contradict each other. However, the paradox simply reminds us that our words about God are poor attempts to express the inexpressible, for 'one can say nothing about God himself that resembles him.'[3] The theology of experience, disclosed by the mystics, is probably much closer to the reality of God precisely because it is born of mystical encounter. Elizabeth responds in kind with the eagerness of a lover, 'We can rise with Him by walking through life "free from all save our love for him."'[4]

'The love I mean, is God's love for us'

Chesterton said that if he could give only one sermon, it would be against pride; Elizabeth's would undoubtedly be on God's love, which is why John Paul II commended Elizabeth of the Trinity to the Church as 'a brilliant witness to the joy of being rooted and grounded in love'.[5] Elizabeth's life and spirituality hinge on this one, awesome reality: she was utterly certain of God's love for her. Nicholl considers there to be no more vital truth in undertaking holiness than the belief that we are loved.[6] Mysticism begins and ends with the experience of being loved and Elizabeth's spiritual journey takes her to the very heart of God's love. There is only one love, God's love for us, and all other loves are only shadows, 'hints and guesses'. Margaret Atwood famously said that, 'The Eskimos had fifty-two names for snow because it was so important to them: there ought to be as many for love', and the counterfeits which masquerade as love are unworthy of the name.

All real love comes from God and leads us back to him. All true love, therefore, is ultimately an expression of God's love, for he is always giving himself even in hidden ways. Wherever we find authentic love, whoever bestows it, however it is expressed, there is God's love, because whoever loves lives in God. Outside of God, there can be no real love; it is not possible, for God is love. The only real authentic love is the love of God for us and in us. Without God, love has lost its mooring.

'Live by love'

Elizabeth was greatly influenced by St Thérèse's spirituality and when asked her ideal of holiness, she responded spontaneously with words from a favourite poem of Thérèse, 'to live by love'.[7] From an early age, Elizabeth had such a wonderful sense of God's love, that sermons on his love moved her to tears. Shortly before entering, Elizabeth was introduced by the Prioress to the Dominican Père Vallée, an inspiring preacher who was also spiritual director to some of the sisters of the Dijon Carmel. She writes:

> The first time I saw him, he spoke of divine charity and I felt over-whelmed by it. Never have I forgotten the impression made on

me by what he said about the infinite love which seeks out and
pursues each soul.[8]

This meeting was pivotal for Elizabeth, who later confided to a
friend that she was so moved by the truths communicated to her
that she wanted him to stop talking so that she could lose herself
in the wonder of God's love. For his part, Père Vallée said it was
a joy to speak to her, 'so pure, so intuitive, and yet so simple,
whose will and intelligence had been given to the Divine Master
from the very first.'[9]

'Thirst for the infinite'

In spite of, or perhaps because of, her naturally affectionate
nature, Elizabeth knew that human love alone could not fulfil her
soul's infinite capacity. Even before entering she wrote, 'He has
placed in my heart a thirst for the infinite and such a great need
for love that He alone can satisfy!'[10] Her Lord did not want her
to 'miss the many-splendour'd thing'.[11] He captivated her with
the immensity of his love and filled her to 'overflowing on all
sides'.[12] Love was her home, her dwelling place, 'I live in love, I
plunge myself into it, and lose myself; it is infinite, the infinity for
which my soul is thirsting.'[13]

Elizabeth was bowled over by God's unconditional, unlimited
love, which became the motivating force behind her radical self-
giving. Juliet's words are so apt for Elizabeth:

> My bounty is as boundless as the sea, my love as deep.
> The more I give thee, the more I have,
> For both are infinite.[14]

The sense of God's infinite love and his boundless generosity
permeates her life and writing, nowhere more exuberantly
expressed than in her letters after profession. Elizabeth is aware
of how much she seemed to have given up, 'from an earthly point
of view'. Inspired by St Thérèse, however, she knew that the
total gift of self is the very essence of love and she fixed her gaze
on Jesus, the 'luminous Star', losing herself in him, 'like a drop
of water in the Ocean'.[15] She had surrendered all and could write

with complete sincerity, 'I delight in the thought of having left all
for Him; it is a joy to give when one loves, and I so love this God
who is jealous of having me for Himself alone.'[16]

Elizabeth's life and joy in this relationship, draw us to listen
for and respond to God's silent invitation, in the depths of our
hearts, 'There, don't you hear it too?/Something is calling . . .'[17]
For Elizabeth, this 'something' is a Someone, the God of Love
who calls to the innermost centre of the soul. When the immensity of our nothingness encounters the immensity of God's limitlessness, there is a divine impact from which, happily, we never
recover.

'God's exceeding love'

For Elizabeth, St Paul's phrase, God's 'exceeding love', captured
the inexpressible mystery of God's limitless love. Steeped in
John of the Cross' two most sublime works, *The Spiritual Canticle* and *The Living Flame of Love*, Elizabeth was wholly convinced
of the supreme importance of God's love, 'What is the use of
anything except the love of God?'[18] Only love matters, 'Love is
the purpose for which He loves.'[19] Firmly believing this she
could say, 'Whatever happens to me is a message or an assurance
of the exceeding love of God; I cannot live my life apart from
that.'[20]

Elizabeth's favourite Scripture texts reveal her fascination with
the sheer lavishness of God's love, particularly Ephesians 2:4
which speaks of God's 'exceeding love', and Galatians 2:20, 'He
loved me and gave himself up for me.' Elizabeth also marvelled at
1 John 4:16, which captures the essence of our faith, 'We have
known and believe the love that God has for us.'[21]

'Always believe in love'

Every child is born with the need to be loved and never outgrows
it. Grace always builds on nature so, inevitably, the Christian life
begins and ends with being loved. Indeed, it only really begins
when we *believe* that we are loved. Pope Benedict's first encyc-
lical, *Deus Caritas Est*, celebrates the God who is love and in his

Introduction to Christianity, he makes the astounding statement, 'only being loved is being saved'.[22] Salvation, therefore, means letting ourselves be loved by God. Van Breeman called this the grace to accept God's acceptance of us, to believe that we are loved deeply and unreservedly:

> Faith is the conviction that God loves us as we are. This is really the core of our faith, and the whole of scripture and all theology are just an elaboration of this. Prayer is our response to this love, basking in it, opening ourselves completely in order to be loved fully by God ... Sin is saying no, I don't need the love you're offering me.[23]

The deep 'knowledge of the saints' is nothing other than the knowledge of God's love. Elizabeth, like St Bernard, affirms belief in God's love as our great act of faith. She muses, 'Will we ever understand how much we are loved?'[24] This love demands a robust faith that sees with God's eyes. In a last letter to Guite, in April 1906, when Elizabeth thought she was dying, and knew how desperately Guite would miss her, she wrote:

> We will always be united, little sister. Always believe in love. If you have to suffer, think you are even *more loved* and always sing thanksgiving. He is so jealous for the beauty of your soul ... That is all He has in view.[25]

For Elizabeth, as for John of the Cross, faith, hope and love are a single reality which not only opens us to God, they actually *give* us God. We are not talking about something sequential, as if we believe, hope and love and then God will respond. No, believing, hoping and loving are encounters with him. They are one whole graced movement towards him, which he empowers us to make. It is crucial to take hold of this radical insight: the very movement of the lips or heart in faith, hope and love give us God. As Augustine exclaims, in the wonderful reading for the Christmas office, 'Is there anything here but grace?'[26]

The profound conviction that suffused Elizabeth's life was the belief in a God who loved her deeply, unconditionally and personally. Herbert's words resonate with sheer wonder at the particularity of God's love:

> My God, what is a heart,
> That thou shouldst it so eye, and woo,
> Pouring upon it all thy art,
> As if thou hadst nothing else to do?[27]

This beautiful evocation of God's tender attentiveness is echoed by Elizabeth, 'You would think He had only me to love and think about from the way He gives Himself to my soul.'[28] This is the way God loves each one of us. This is the love she asks us to believe in, live in and delight in.

Love-Filled Letters

Elizabeth's belief in God's love never lost its freshness and her enthusiasm spills over in her letters. They convey her warm, deeply affectionate nature as she zealously shares her insights into all things holy, especially God's love, combining human and spiritual in a wonderful synthesis. She rejoiced at being called to live in relationship with this 'Being who is Love' and urges her correspondents to place God's love at the centre of their lives. The Holy Spirit continues to work through her letters which have immense vitality, and when we read them as if addressed to us personally, we feel their spiritual force even more. Elizabeth manages to draw us into the sacred space she inhabits, holding us close to God by her believing. She encourages us to surrender ourselves and all our cares to God, 'who envelops us in his love.'[29] We hear echoes of Julian of Norwich, who speaks of being 'enfolded in God's love', totally wrapped around, held in God's secure, loving embrace.[30]

After Elizabeth's death, her mother testified, 'Anyone who thinks that the cloister narrows the heart should get to know this Carmelite who went on loving in times of both joy and sorrow.'[31] On the contrary, from the moment she entered, Elizabeth's correspondence radiates an infectious enthusiasm for her Carmelite life which increasingly broadens her spiritual horizons and expands her heart. For Elizabeth, the sole occupation of the Carmelite is to love and pray through everything, and she expressed her love as prayer which overflowed into her letters.

Writing at night during the time of the great silence after Compline, Elizabeth frequently concluded with a promise to carry those she loved with her to prayer, 'The bell is about to call me to Matins, I leave you without leaving you, for I carry you in my soul, close to the One who is all Love.'[32] This time of solitude, which Elizabeth so cherished, became a time of deepening and merging loves: love for God, love for family and friends, love for the Church and her suffering country, for all love is one and no one is excluded. From the sacredness of her Carmelite cell she gives new meaning to Donne's claim, 'love . . . makes one little room an everywhere.' [33]

Writing to her dear friend, Canon Angles, on the first anniversary of entering Carmel, Elizabeth pours out her heart, full of thanksgiving and joy, amazed by God's love:

> Why has He loved me so much? . . . I feel so full of misery, but I love Him; that is all I know how to do, I love Him with His own love . . . When I feel my God invade my whole soul, as I pray to Him for you, it seems to me that it is a prayer He cannot resist, and I want Him to make me all-powerful![34]

Through the struggles and sufferings of her noviciate, Elizabeth acquired a strong sense of her own misery and the fragility of the human condition. Rather than this becoming an obstacle to God's love, she continued to love and trust him, sensing that only God could free her from her limitations and misery. Knowing our nothingness before God brings freedom, not dejection; it places us in the truth, liberates us from the weight of our own and others' unreal and crushing expectations, bringing us into the peacefulness of humility:

> The only wisdom we can hope to acquire
> Is the wisdom of humility: humility is endless.[35]

Elizabeth recognized that God is always the protagonist and was reassured by John of the Cross' consoling words, 'It should be known that if a person is seeking God, his beloved is seeking him much more.'[36] God gives us the capacity to receive his love; he loves us into the power of loving him. Elizabeth knew that God's love and her response were both his gift, and she was overcome with gratitude.

A characteristic of love is that we become like those we love, be they human or divine. When God loves us, something astonishing happens, 'With God, to love the soul is to put her somehow in Himself and make her His equal. Thus He loves the soul . . . with the very love by which He loves Himself.'[37] Elizabeth marvelled that God loved in her and prayed in her, making her love and prayer so powerful that, as John of the Cross says, 'a little of this pure love is more precious to God and the soul and more beneficial to the Church, even though it seems one is doing nothing, than all these other works put together',[38] thus expressing the deepest rationale of the contemplative life.

For Elizabeth, nothing is outside God's love, nothing, and like all lovers, her prose becomes poetic when she reflects on this all-encompassing love:

> Ask Him to make me live for love alone: this is my vocation . . .
> let us wake in love, let us surrender ourselves to love all day long
> by doing the will of the good God, in His sight, with Him, in
> Him, for Him alone; let us give ourselves ceaselessly in whatever
> way He wishes; then, when evening comes, after an endless
> dialogue of love in our heart, let us sleep in love. Perhaps we will
> see our faults and infidelities; let us abandon them to love which
> is a consuming fire.[39]

Her words are an invitation and a prayer. Convinced that God offers his love to all, she longed for others to share her understanding. This is her great gift to the Church, and surely one of her most powerful words: her belief and delight in God's 'exceeding love'. This is no exalted spirituality, it is how we are all called to live, but we forget so easily; when we look to Elizabeth, she reminds us who we are and what life is about.

'Secrets for our Reverend Mother'[40]

All that Elizabeth had learned about God's love came to fruition during the last nine months of her life, spent in the infirmary, under the care of Mother Germaine. During this period their relationship shifted to a quasi-mystical level, with Elizabeth the 'host-victim' and Mother Germaine her 'consecrating priest'.[41] Their sacramental relationship provides a valuable model for the sick and their carers, for perhaps only those who have ministered to the seriously ill and the dying can fully understand the sacredness of the bond that is formed.

Just before she died, Elizabeth, barely able to hold a pen, struggled to write a farewell letter to comfort Mother Germaine. One can only begin to imagine Mother Germaine's reaction on receiving this profound message after Elizabeth's death. Only in 1934, after Mother Germaine's death, was this letter discovered inside a well-worn envelope, tucked in her Carmelite Book of Prayers. It bore the solemn words, 'Secrets for our Reverend Mother', and there was a broken red seal on the back of the envelope. Elizabeth's final words disclose the depth of her loving intimacy with God and her desire to lead Mother Germaine to a deeper relationship with him.

Who was this sister who inspired such love and devotion in Elizabeth? Mother Germaine's obituary describes her as an outstanding Carmelite who had been elected Prioress of the Dijon Carmel eight times. She was a deeply spiritual religious possessed of exceptional talents; a gifted leader, much loved by her sisters. However, fearful of her inability to fulfil her responsibilities, she lacked confidence and struggled with feelings of inadequacy.

Elizabeth wanted to affirm and reassure her Prioress, but not merely with her own words or ideas. Only after 'hours of profound recollection and unifying contact' did Elizabeth begin to write, revealing what she believed God had 'helped her to understand'. Her words are thus invested with the power that only comes from remaining in the Lord's presence; she speaks from her inner sanctuary and we sense the sacredness of this message of love. She, therefore, confidently encouraged Mother Germaine to read this letter as coming from God, indeed, as the very voice of God. Elizabeth knew that she would have crossed the threshold of eternity when this letter was read and, only in the light of this, can her message be fully understood. Although originally destined for Mother Germaine, its message is timeless, reaching out to each one of us.

'You are uncommonly loved!'

Elizabeth opens with an exclamation which speaks directly to our heart's need: 'You are uncommonly loved!' 'Uncommonly' as in especially, exceptionally, singularly, rarely, surprisingly, amazingly, uniquely . . . the list goes on. We need to savour each word in order to draw out all the richness of the statement because, paradoxically, we resist that which we most desire: to be loved with a preferential love. Victor Hugo says that 'the supreme happiness of life is the conviction that we are loved – loved for ourselves, or rather, loved in spite of ourselves', and that is just on a human level. Only God can love us unconditionally, only then are we loved by a love we never dared hope for.

'Let yourself be loved'

In this special letter, Elizabeth takes the Jesus-Peter dialogue from chapter 21 of John's Gospel and turns it on its head. Instead of Jesus' question, 'Do you love me more than these?' painfully recalling Peter's betrayal and failure, comes the completely unexpected, '*Let* yourself be loved more than these,' spoken not once, by the Master, but three times. Elizabeth visibly enlarged the word '*Let*' each time to emphasize her message. God wants to love us, but he respects us too much to force himself on us; we have to allow him to love us, we have to let him in. In *Mister God,* Anna grasps the magnitude of God's graciousness, expressed in his waiting and longing for us:

> We are at our own centre. Even though he is at the centre of all things, he waits outside and knocks to come in. It is we who open the door. Mister God doesn't break it down and come in, no, he

knocks and waits. 'It makes me very important, don't it, Fynn?
Fancy Mister God taking second place!' that's the heart of free
will.[42]

What we each need and want most in life is to love and be loved
and Elizabeth shows that Christ's love is the answer: 'Let yourself
be loved.' Elizabeth repeats this invitation six times, over and
over again, so that it penetrates our very being.

'This love can rebuild what has been destroyed'

Elizabeth anticipates and dispels any possible objections.
Although Christ freely pours out his love, actually allowing
ourselves to be loved is probably the most difficult thing we can
do. We are so hard on ourselves, never satisfied, always feeling
we could do better. It is uncomfortable to stand before God as we
are, with our weaknesses, struggles and imperfections. Fear and
insecurity often paralyze us, which is why we need to hear the
refrain, over and over again, 'Let yourself be loved ... Let yourself be loved,' by a love that recreates. Gradually, almost imperceptibly, defences are steadily worn down; our resistance turns to
longing, and disbelief is transformed into acceptance.

What happens if we have been deeply hurt and damaged? I
think that Elizabeth is giving us a way through. We cannot deny
the pain, but we can bring it to God who is waiting to love and
heal us for, 'the soul's health is the love of God'.[43] The Old
Testament word for truth, *emeth*, means the reliability of God's
love. The most basic, foundational truth in life is that God loves
us and we can rely on him unconditionally. We can almost hear
Elizabeth saying, 'let him in, let him love you, let yourself be
loved.' Repeating these healing words is like being caressed by
the tenderness of God, reassuring, comforting, loving us.

'He will do everything'

Mother Germaine's insecurity probably made her feel that this
overwhelming love could not possibly apply to her. Perhaps we
have the same sense of our unworthiness in the face of God's love,

but Elizabeth insists that God's love will accomplish all, 'He will do everything in you. He will go right to the end', because that is what love means. Elizabeth knows that, of ourselves, we can do nothing either to earn or to attract his grace. That is not the point, God's love is the determiner and God's love knows no limits.

'Love is your vocation'

We cannot stop God loving. We cannot limit him for 'love is his meaning', and his love is our meaning.[44] 'Let yourself be loved', by a love that heals and transforms. Then we are freed to live in, and from, the depths of our soul. Elizabeth's life was suffused with the wonder of God's overflowing, unlimited, extravagant love and she conveys this message with the authority and conviction that only comes from lived experience. We find her message so compelling because it is a truth we need and long to hear: our vocation is to be loved by God.

Elizabeth encourages us to listen to what Christ is saying, 'Let yourself be loved ... That is your vocation; in being faithful to it you will make me happy because you will thus magnify the power of my love.' Only God's love matters. My vocation lies in letting God love me. God needs those who are receptive to the love he is offering. What a beautiful calling: in letting God love us, we receive love for the Church and the world, for those who do not know they even need his love. Thérèse understood her vocation 'to be love in the heart of the Church.' Elizabeth understood hers to 'be loved in the heart of the Church.'

'In communion with Love'

Elizabeth daringly affirms that she understands God's plan for Mother Germaine and promises to instruct her so that she will profit from her vision. There is such confidence in her writing, that she inspires confidence in her reader.

Elizabeth invites Mother Germaine to allow her to live in her, promising to keep her believing in God's love. She says that Mother Germaine's belief in God's love will be a sign that she is 'dwelling' in her soul: when she thinks of Elizabeth, she will be reminded to believe in God's love and let him love her. When we allow others to love us we free them to be associated in his work and allow him to love us through them. Letting others help us is also a way of loving them. This is a challenging idea. So often, our independence and self-sufficiency keep others at bay, making them feel either inferior or redundant because we do not seem to need their help. This keeps us safe from the risks of loving and being loved, for when we love, we open ourselves to the possibility of rejection, and this hurts. However, we also prevent ourselves experiencing the joy and wonder of love. This is what we are called to; our vocation is to receive love and to be that unconditional love for others. God loves us through others and he loves others through us. Elizabeth longs to keep us 'in communion with love'.

'Be faithful to love'

Elizabeth reassures us that the only fidelity the Master requires is the fidelity of remaining in communion with Love. This covers everything as, 'the real talent [is] to remain in God. It alone is the core.'[45] Without this, everything else is insignificant. You will 'never be commonplace if you are vigilant in love!' What a marvellous statement: the basis of our worth is our dignity as beloved sons and daughters of God. We are loved uniquely, personally and profoundly, and our only real 'work' in life is to 'let ourselves be loved.' This applies to all people, especially all Christians. Our importance is not determined by what we have or do, but by the fact that we are made in the image and likeness of God. Love is written into our very nature.

What is more astonishing is Elizabeth's assertion that, at our worst moments, God loves us even *more*. Our bad days thereby become our best days. At those times when all we long for is the welcome oblivion of sleep, God is there, longing to love, hold and support us. All we have to do is to let him in, 'believe in His love'. Believing through darkness makes us even *more* loved, because it is so much harder to believe when we feel demoralized and out of sorts. This draws God's love even more. Faith in his love changes everything.

In this letter, Elizabeth is calling to us, crying to us, sharing her own profound awareness of God's wonderful, abundant love. He is there, waiting, longing, only hoping that we will 'let ourselves be loved.' Nowhere in the history of Christian spirituality has this core insight been expressed with such clarity, conviction and intensity.

Some months before she died, Elizabeth confided to her mother that St Paul's phrase, 'he has loved us exceedingly', was like a 'summary of [her] life and could be written on every one of its moments'.[46] There is a beautiful passage, in a letter to Canon Angles, which parallels the 'Hymn to Charity' in 1 Corinthians. Elizabeth expresses her experience of God's love in the lyrical language of lover and mystic, and we feel the 'lifetime burning in every moment': [47]

Elizabeth's Hymn to Love

It is so good to give when one loves, and I love Him so much,
  this God who is jealous of having me all for Himself.
    I feel so much love over my soul,
      it is like an Ocean I immerse and lose myself in:
        it is my vision on earth while I am waiting
          for the face-to-face vision in light.
            He is in me, I am in Him.
    I have only to love Him, to let myself be loved,
        all the time, through all things:
  to wake in Love, to move in Love, to sleep in Love,
      my soul in His Soul, my heart in His Heart,
  my eyes in His eyes, so that through His contact
    He may purify me, free me from my misery.
        If you knew how it fills me.[48]

Notes

1. *L* 269; *LR* 10–11.
2. *L* 199.
3. *C* 26.4.
4. *L* 199.
5. John Paul II, *Homily for the Beatification of Elizabeth of the Trinity*.
6. Nicholl, *Holiness*, p. 38.
7. *Reminiscences*, p. 73.

8. Ibid., p. 55.
9. Ibid., p. 56.
10. *L* 169.
11. F. Thompson, 'In No Strange Land', *LOH* III, 801*.
12. *L* 199.
13. *Reminiscences,* p. 90.
14. Shakespeare, *Romeo and Juliet* 2.2.133–5.
15. *L* 190.
16. *L* 177.
17. 'Calling' in *Ghosts*, John Fuller.
18. *3A* 30.5.
19. *C* 32.5.
20. *Reminiscences,* p. 90.
21. *L* 239.
22. Ratzinger, *Introduction to Christianity*, p. 74.
23. Van Breeman, *Called by Name*, p. 9, see p. 73.
24. *L* 191.
25. *L* 269.
26. Augustine, Sermon 185, *LOH* I, p. 171.
27. Sheldrake, *The Spirituality of George Herbert*, p. 33.
28. *L* 275, see *LF* 2.36.
29. *L* 129.
30. *Julian of Norwich*, chs. 6 and 10.
31. Dijon Carmel, *Amour Excessif,* DVD.
32. *L* 94.
33. 'The Good-Morrow', *John Donne The Complete English Poems*, p. 60.
34. *L* 131.
35. Eliot, 'East Coker', *Four Quartets*, l. 98.
36. *LF* 3.28. See *1A* 1.4.
37. *C* 32.6.
38. *C* 29.2.
39. *L* 172.
40. All quotations in this section are from *L* 337, unless indicated otherwise.
41. *L* 306, see *L* 320.
42. Fynn, *Mister God*, p. 179.
43. *C* 11.11.
44. *Julian of Norwich*, ch. 86.
45. Van Breeman, *Called by Name*, p. 117.
46. *L* 280.
47. Eliot, 'East Coker', *Four Quartets*, ll. 139–40.
48. *L* 177.

Prayer to the Trinity

O my God, Trinity whom I adore; help me to forget myself entirely that I may be established in You as still and as peaceful as if my soul were already in eternity. May nothing trouble my peace or make me leave You, O my Unchanging One, but may each minute carry me further into the depths of Your mystery.

Give peace to my soul make it Your heaven, Your beloved dwelling and Your resting place. May I never leave You there alone but be wholly present, my faith wholly vigilant, wholly adoring and wholly surrendered to Your creative action.

O My beloved Christ, crucified by love, I wish to be a bride for Your Heart; I wish to cover You with glory; I wish to love You . . . even unto death! But I feel my weakness, and I ask You to 'clothe me with Yourself', to identify my soul with all the movements of Your Soul, to overwhelm me, to possess me, to substitute Yourself for me that my life may be but a radiance of Your Life. Come into me as Adorer, as Restorer, as Saviour.

Eternal Word, Word of my God, I want to spend my life in listening to You, to become wholly teachable that I may learn all from You. Then, through all nights, all voids, all helplessness, I want to gaze on You and always remain in Your great light. O my beloved Star, so fascinate me that I may not withdraw from Your radiance.

Consuming Fire, Spirit of Love, 'come upon me', and create in my soul a kind of incarnation of the Word: that I may be another humanity for Him in which He can renew His whole Mystery. And You, O Father, bend lovingly over Your poor little creature; 'cover her with your shadow', seeing in her only the 'Beloved in whom You are well pleased.'

My Three, my All, my Beatitude, infinite Solitude, Immensity in which I lose myself, I surrender myself to You as your prey. Bury Yourself in me that I may bury myself in You until I depart to contemplate in Your light the abyss of Your greatness.

'Praise of Glory'

Heaven in Faith

A 'Praise of Glory'

(Written to console and encourage her sister, Guite, this is a beautiful, lyrical meditation on the meaning of the vocation of a 'Praise of Glory'.)

Heaven in Faith

We have been predestined by the decree of Him who works all things according to the counsel of His will, so that we may be the praise of His glory.

It is St Paul who tells us this, St Paul who was instructed by God Himself. How do we realize this great dream of the Heart of our God, this immutable will for our souls? In a word, how do we correspond to our vocation and become perfect 'Praises of Glory of the Most Holy Trinity'?

In Heaven, each soul is a praise of glory of the Father, the Word, and the Holy Spirit, for each soul is established in pure love and lives no longer its own life, but the life of God. Then it knows Him, St Paul says, as it is known by Him. In other words, 'its intellect is the intellect of God, its will the will of God, its love the very love of God. In reality it is the Spirit of love and of strength who transforms the soul, for to Him it has been given to supply what is lacking to the soul,' as St Paul says again, 'He works in it this glorious transformation.' St John of the Cross affirms that 'the soul surrendered to love, through the strength of the Holy Spirit, is not far from being raised to the degree of which we have just spoken,' even here below! This is what I call a perfect 'Praise of Glory'!

A 'Praise of Glory' is a soul that lives in God, that loves Him with a pure and disinterested love, without seeking itself in the sweetness of this love; that loves Him beyond all His gifts and even though it would not have received anything from Him, it desires the good of the Object thus loved. Now how do we effectively desire and will good to God if not in accomplishing His will since this will orders everything for His greater glory? Thus, the soul must surrender itself to this will completely, passionately, so as to will nothing else but what God wills.

A 'Praise of Glory' is a soul of silence that remains like a lyre under the mysterious touch of the Holy Spirit, that He may draw from it divine harmonies; it knows that suffering is a string that produces still more beautiful sounds; so it loves to see this string on its instrument that it may more delightfully move the Heart of its God.

A 'Praise of Glory' is a soul that gazes on God in faith and simplicity; it is a reflector of all that He is; it is like a bottomless abyss into which He can flow and expand; it is also like a crystal through which He can radiate and contemplate all His perfections and His own splendour. A soul which thus permits the divine Being to satisfy in itself His need to communicate 'all that He is and all that He has,' is in reality the praise of glory of all His gifts.

Finally, a 'Praise of Glory' is one who is always giving thanks. Each of her acts, her movements, her thoughts, her aspirations, at the same time that they are rooting her more deeply in love, are like an echo of the eternal Sanctus.

In the Heaven of glory the blessed have no rest 'day or night, saying: Holy, holy, holy is the Lord God Almighty . . . They fall down and worship Him who lives forever and ever.'

In the heaven of her soul, the 'Praise of glory' has already begun her work of eternity. Her song is uninterrupted, for she is under the action of the Holy Spirit who effects everything in her; and although she is not always aware of it, for the weakness of nature does not allow her to be established in God without distractions, she always sings, she always adores, for she has, so to speak, wholly passed into praise and love in her passion for the glory of her God. In the heaven of our soul let us be praises of glory of the Holy Trinity, praises of love of our Immaculate Mother. One day the veil will fall, we will be introduced into the eternal courts, and there we will sing in the bosom of infinite Love. And God will give us 'the new name promised to the Victor.' What will it be?

LAUDEM GLORIAE

Bibliography

Scripture

The Jerusalem Bible, Standard Version, (London: Darton, Longman & Todd, 1966).

Church Documents

Catechism of the Catholic Church (London: Geoffrey Chapman, 1997).

Catholic Bishops' Conference of England and Wales; Catholic Bishops' Conference of Scotland, *The Gift of Scripture* (London: Catholic Truth Society, 2005).

Divine Office, The Liturgy of the Hours According to the Roman Rite (London-Glasgow: Collins; Sydney: E. J. Dwyer; Dublin: Talbot, 2001).

John Paul II, *Homily for the Beatification of Elizabeth of the Trinity,* (Vatican, 25 November, 1984).

John Paul II, *Novo Millennio Ineunte* (London: CTS, 2001).

John Paul II, *Salvifici Doloris* (London: CTS, 1984).

Paul VI, *Mysterium Fidei* (London: CTS, 1965).

Vatican II, *Gaudium et Spes* (London: CTS, 1965).

Vatican II, *Lumen Gentium* (London: CTS, 1964).

Primary Bibliography

Balthasar, H. U. von, *Two Sisters in the Spirit: Thérèse of Lisieux and Elizabeth of the Trinity* (San Francisco: Ignatius Press, 1992).

Bancroft, A., (trans.), *Barb of Fire: Twenty Poems of Blessed Elizabeth of the Trinity with selected passages from Blessed Columba Marmion* (Leominster: Gracewing, 2001).

De Meester, C., (ed.), *Élisabeth de la Trinité: Oeuvres Complètes* (Paris: Cerf, 2002).

Dijon Carmel, *Sr Elizabeth of the Trinity's Death Circular* (Private Publication, 1906).

Dijon Carmel, *Reminiscences of Sr Elizabeth of the Trinity Servant of God,* A Benedictine of Stanbrook Abbey, (trans.), (Cork: Mercier Press, 1913).

Dijon Carmel, *Mother Germaine's Death Circular* (Private Publication, 1935).

Kavanaugh, K. and Rodriguez, O., (trans.), *The Collected Works of St Teresa of Avila,* vols I-III, Second Revised Edition, (Washington: ICS, 1976).

Kavanaugh, K. and Rodriguez, O., (trans.), *The Collected Works of St John of the Cross,* Second Edition, (Washington: ICS, 1979).

Moorcroft, J., *He is My Heaven: The Life of Elizabeth of the Trinity* (Washington: ICS, 2001).

Murphy, M. T., *Elizabeth of the Trinity: Always Believe in Love, Selected Spiritual Writings* (New York: New City Press, 2009).

Philipon, M. M., *The Spiritual Doctrine of Sr Elizabeth of the Trinity* (Cork: Mercier Press, 1947).

General Bibliography

Arendup, M. E., trans., *A Carmelite of the Sacred Heart: The Life of Mother Marie of Jesus* (London: Burns, Oates & Washbourne, 1923).

Bloom, A., *God and Man* (London: Hodder & Stoughton, 1971).

Chesterton, G. K., *Orthodoxy* (London: Fontana, 1908).

Corbishley, T., (trans.), *The Spiritual Exercises of Saint Ignatius* (Wheathampstead: Anthony Clarke, 1963).

Eliot, T. S., *Four Quartets* (London: Faber and Faber, 1974).

Eliot, T. S., *Selected Poems* (London: Faber and Faber, 1964).

Frankl, V., *Man's Search for Meaning* (London: Hodder and Stoughton, 1964).

Fuller, J., *Ghosts* (London: Chatto &Windus, 2004).

Fynn, *Mister God, This is Anna* (London: Collins, 1974).

Gardner, W. H., *Gerard Manley Hopkins Selected Poems and Prose* (London: Penguin Books, 1953).

Hildebrand, D. von, *Transformation in Christ* (San Francisco: Ignatius Press, 1948).

Hillesum, E., *An Interrupted Life: The Diaries and Letters of Etty*

Hillesum (London: Persephone Books Ltd, 1999).

Hume, B., *The Mystery of the Cross* (London: DLT, 1998).

Julian of Norwich, *Revelations of Divine Love* (London: Penguin Classics, 1966).

Kierkegaard, S., *Purity of Heart is to Will One Thing,* (Steere, D., trans.), (London: Fontana, 1961).

Kinney, D., 'Guite – The Sister of Elizabeth of the Trinity', in *Carmelite Digest*, vol. 20, no. 4, Winter 2005.

Laird, M., *Into the Silent Land* (London: DLT, 2006).

Maloney, G., *Prayer of the Heart* (Notre Dame, IN: Ave Maria Press, 1981).

Merton, T., *Elected Silence* (London: Hollis and Carter, 1949).

Murray Elwood, J., *Kindly Light: The Spiritual Vision of John Henry Newman* (Notre Dame, IN: Ave Maria Press, 1979).

Newman, J. H., *Parochial and Plain Sermons,* vols. I-VIII (London: Longmans Green and Co., 1896).

Nicholl, D., *Holiness* (London: DLT, 1981).

Otto, R., *The Idea of the Holy* (Oxford: OUP, 1923).

Radcliffe, T., *Seven Last Words* (London: Burns & Oates, 2004).

Rahner, K., *On Prayer* (New York: Paulist Press, 1958).

Ratzinger, J., *Introduction to Christianity* (London: Burns & Oates, 1969).

Ratzinger, J. (Benedict XVI, Pope), *Jesus of Nazareth* (London: Bloomsbury, 2007).

Rolheiser, R., *Against an Infinite Horizon* (London: Hodder & Stoughton, 1995).

Sheldrake, P., *Love Took My Hand: The Spirituality of George Herbert* (London: DLT, 2000).

Smith, A. J., *John Donne: The Complete English Poems* (London: Penguin, 1971).

Somervell, D. C., *Selections from Wordsworth* (London: J. M. Dent and Sons, 1920).

Squire, A., *Asking the Fathers* (London: SPCK, 1973).

Teilhard de Chardin, P., *Le Milieu Divin* (London: Collins, 1960).

Tranvik, M. D., 'Luther on Baptism', in *Lutheran Quarterly*, vol. XIII, 1999.

Underhill, E., *Mysticism: The Nature and Development of Spiritual Consciousness* (London: Methuen & Co. Ltd, 1911).

Underhill, E., *The Spiritual Life* (Harrisburg, PA: Morehouse, 1984).

Van Breeman, P. G., *Called By Name* (Denville, NJ: Dimension Books, 1976).

Vorgrimler, H., *Sacramental Theology* (Collegeville: The Liturgical Press, 1992).

Weil, S. E., *Waiting on God,* (Craufurd, E., trans.), (London: Harper & Row, 1951).

Williams, C., (ed.), *The Letters of Evelyn Underhill*, (Westminster, MD: Christian Classics, 1989).

CDs and DVDs

Dijon Carmel, *Élisabeth de la Trinité Un Amour Excessif; Elizabeth of the Trinity, Boundless Love,* (DVD, 2006).

Manservigi, M., *Sabeth: Élisabeth de la Trinité 1880–1906,* (Carmel of Dijon DVD, 2006).

Two sets of CDs of talks on Elizabeth of the Trinity, given by the author and recorded live are available from: Carmelite Monastery, Honeysgreen Lane, Liverpool, L12 9HY United Kingdom; or email: livcarm@hotmail.co.uk

Set 1 – 2007
Talk 1 Elizabeth of the Trinity – Life and Spirituality Before Carmel
Talk 2 Elizabeth of the Trinity – Life and Spirituality in Carmel
Talk 3 Elizabeth of the Trinity's Spirituality

Set 2 – 2008
Talk 1 Elizabeth of the Trinity – Baptismal and Trinitarian Spirituality
Talk 2 Elizabeth of the Trinity – Eucharistic Spirituality
Talk 3 Elizabeth of the Trinity's Teaching on Prayer
Talk 4 Elizabeth of the Trinity and St Paul